ORGANIZATION AND GOVERNANCE USING ALGORITHMS

DIGITAL ACTIVISM AND SOCIETY: POLITICS, ECONOMY AND CULTURE IN NETWORK COMMUNICATION.

The *Digital Activism and Society: Politics, Economy and Culture in Network Communication* series focuses on the political use of digital everyday-networked media by corporations, governments, international organizations (Digital Politics), as well as civil society actors, NGOs, activists, social movements, and dissidents (Digital Activism) attempting to recruit, organize and fund their operations, through information communication technologies.

The series publishes books on theories and empirical case studies of digital politics and activism in the specific context of communication networks. Topics covered by the series include, but are not limited to:

- the different theoretical and analytical approaches of political communication in digital networks;
- studies of sociopolitical media movements and activism (and "hacktivism");
- transformations of older topics such as inequality, gender, class, power, identity, and group belonging;
- strengths and vulnerabilities of social networks.

Series Editor

Professor Athina Karatzogianni

About the Series Editor

Athina Karatzogianni is Professor of Media and Communication at the University of Leicester. Her research looks at media theory, global politics and resistance networks.

Published Books in This Series

Digital Materialism: Origins, Philosophies, Prospects by Baruch Gottlieb

Nirbhaya, New Media and Digital Gender Activism by Adrija Dey

Digital Life on Instagram: New Social Communication of Photography by Elisa Serafinelli

Internet Oligopoly: The Corporate Takeover of Our Digital World by Nikos Smyrnaios

Digital Activism and Cyberconflicts in Nigeria: Occupy Nigeria, Boko Haram and MEND by Shola A. Olabode

Platform Economics: Rhetoric and Reality in the "Sharing Economy" by Cristiano Codagnone

Communication as Gesture: Media(tion), Meaning, & Movement by Michael Schandorf

Chinese Social Media: Face, Sociality, and Civility by Shuhan Chen and Peter Lunt

Posthumanism in Digital Culture: Cyborgs, Gods and Fandom by Callum T.F. McMillan

Media, Technology and Education in a Post-Truth Society: From Fake News, Datafication and Mass Surveillance to the Death of Trust by Alex Grech

3D Printing Cultures, Politics and Hackerspaces by Leandros Savvides

Environmental Security in Greece: Perceptions From Industry, Government, NGOs and the Public by Charis(Harris) Gerosideris

Fantasy, Neoliberalism and Precariousness: Coping Strategies in the Cultural Industries by Jérémy Vachet

Crisis Communication in China: Strategies Taken by the Chinese Government and Online Public Opinion by Wei Cui

Digital Politics, Digital Histories, Digital Futures: New Approaches for Historicising, Politicising and Imagining the Digital by Adi Kuntsman and Liu Xin

Digital Memory in Brazil: A Fragmented and Elastic Negationist Remembrance of the Dictatorship by Leda Balbino

Forthcoming Titles

Duty to Revolt: Transnational and Commemorative Aspects of Revolution by George Souvlis and Athina Karatzogianni

Fractal Leadership: The Technosocial Transformation of Leadership in Social Movements by Athina Karatzogianni and Jacob Matthews

Massively Marginal: Kuaishou as China's Subaltern Platform by Dino Ge Zhang, Jian Xu and Gabriele de Seta

ORGANIZATION AND GOVERNANCE USING ALGORITHMS

BY

IOANNIS AVRAMOPOULOS
RelationalAI, Inc, USA

United Kingdom – North America – Japan – India
Malaysia – China

Emerald Publishing Limited
Emerald Publishing, Floor 5, Northspring, 21-23 Wellington Street, Leeds LS1 4DL

First edition 2024

Copyright © 2024 Ioannis Avramopoulos.
Published under exclusive licence by Emerald Publishing Limited.

Reprints and permissions service
Contact: www.copyright.com

No part of this book may be reproduced, stored in a retrieval system, transmitted in any form or by any means electronic, mechanical, photocopying, recording or otherwise without either the prior written permission of the publisher or a licence permitting restricted copying issued in the UK by The Copyright Licensing Agency and in the USA by The Copyright Clearance Center. Any opinions expressed in the chapters are those of the authors. Whilst Emerald makes every effort to ensure the quality and accuracy of its content, Emerald makes no representation implied or otherwise, as to the chapters' suitability and application and disclaims any warranties, express or implied, to their use.

British Library Cataloguing in Publication Data
A catalogue record for this book is available from the British Library

ISBN: 978-1-83797-061-2 (Print)
ISBN: 978-1-83797-060-5 (Online)
ISBN: 978-1-83797-062-9 (Epub)

Printed and bound by CPI Group (UK) Ltd, Croydon, CR0 4YY

INVESTOR IN PEOPLE

CONTENTS

Preface ix
Acknowledgments xi

1. Introduction 1
2. On the Cognitive Foundation of Organization 9
3. Organizational Systems Design Requirements 23
4. The Stigmata of Unaccountable Presence 41
5. Organization Based on Accountably Anonymous Delegation 69
6. Concluding Remarks and Future Work 85

References 93

PREFACE

In this book, we attempt to ground the organization of production of goods and services on a sound mathematical foundation. To that end, we develop an algorithmic theory of organizational governance wherein the individual contributing to organizational output is a first-order principal (in a fashion similar to how players are first-order principals in game theory). Our theory is in sharp contrast to the institution of hierarchical delegation that plagues organizations. Our main contribution is an organizational primitive we call *accountably anonymous delegation* based on which we design a pair of institutional mechanisms that can replace hierarchies. Our perspective and ideas are deeply ingrained in the foundations of Greek thought and are significantly influenced by modern American culture. The driver for this inquiry is the ongoing European crisis (but my thinking predates it).

ACKNOWLEDGMENTS

I would like to thank Professor Athina Karatzogianni whose comments helped improve the quality of this manuscript. I would also like to thank local coffee shops in Melissia, especially Abbaeion, for their hospitality.

1

INTRODUCTION

1.1 THE FLAWED INSTITUTIONAL FOUNDATION OF ORGANIZATIONS

Gold Guns Girls

$\qquad\qquad\qquad\qquad\qquad\qquad\qquad\qquad$ –METRIC

Organization is ideologically oriented toward visions of *gold* and *bondage*. I use the term *gold* to express a desire for wealth and success (as in *gold medals* in sports competitions). I use the term *bondage* to express stimulating bondage be that organizational or erotic: Organizations are about fulfilling our dreams and erotic intimacy is certainly within the dreams that motivate us to have good performance in organizational tasks. (The idea that "bondage" plays a major role in organization dates back to Jean-Jacques Rousseau – see beginning of his famous book *The social contract:* "Man is born free, and everywhere he is in chains.") In this book, a centerpiece of my discussion is hierarchical protocols of organization. Organizations are rife with hierarchical structures, which negatively affect organizational performance and the emotional experience of actors that partake in these structures. I discuss delegation hierarchies from an analytical perspective scrutinizing the elementary principles of their operation and how they can be harmful to our societies. I later draw on this discussion to design organizational methods at the antipodal bank of hierarchies.

1.1.1 Organization as the Production of Goods and Services

The main characteristic of an organization is an effort to reap the benefits of *coordination opportunities*, that is, situations whereby a coordinated effort to produce goods or services brings more benefits to the respective organizational actors than what they would have received otherwise. To that end, an organization leverages individuals and an institutional and hardware infrastructure. Since effort is a computational phenomenon, it is meaningful to model an organization as a distributed computing system (where organizational actors are computing elements), but caution is required to adopt such perspective: Modeling an individual as a Turing machine (as in the standard model of distributed computing) is an approximation (e.g., the Church-Turing thesis is an unsettled thesis in theoretical computer science). Nevertheless viewing organizational actors as processors that communicate through a shared infrastructure (physical and virtual) is a meaningful approximation.

1.1.2 Profit Maximization as a Goal of Corporate Organization

A defining characteristic of corporate organizations is that they often set profit maximization as a primary objective of their operation (interested, as management is, on share profit). That is, profit maximization often receives priority over other objectives in the synthesis of optimal products and services. Of course what is optimal from the perspective of product or service design naturally depends on who buys such a product or service. That said, it is often the case that organizations prefer to look for affluent customers (willing to spend important amounts on purchases) and optimize the experience of those customers at the possible expense of other, less affluent, customers, the organization's own employees, and the environment. Thus, profit maximization gives rise to *negative externalities* in an organization's operation process. In the recent history of humanity, these externalities started becoming conspicuously visible with the advent of the industrial age.

1.1.3 The Negative Externalities of Industrialization

Industrialization has indisputably come at a cost of magnitude that is not only visible but substantial enough to impress projections of a possible decline of human civilization in its entirety, if not of the complete annihilation of humans from the face of the planet: Industrialization has degraded the quality of the terrestrial nature hosting us. From the perspective of economic theory, the reasons for this negative effect of industrial activity on the very same entities that strive to support the industrialization efforts (theoretically promising to advance their living standards), namely, the individual actors, are not to be ascribed to a fundamental flaw of human nature such as "greed" as unconscionable voices like to purport, but rather a manifestation of a simple phenomenon, well-studied in economic theory, namely, that of (the aforementioned) negative externalities (effects of possibly "optimal" decisions that, in trying to optimize artificial objectives such as *profit*, negatively influence the decisions through mechanisms external to the objective function being optimized).

Environmental detriments resulting from industrial production can, for example, be addressed by "internalizing" the environmental impact of polluting industry through international regulation (as it affects the competitiveness of national economies in global markets). This is difficult.

In this book, I argue that *poverty and inequality* in Western societies (such as that of the United States, for example) can be attributed to a similar phenomenon of *organizational pollution* having the same roots and analogous implications in its detrimental effects as industrial pollution has on the natural environment. These phenomena can be traced to negative externalities in the decisions of national states, corporations, and individuals, that manifest in internal mechanisms of operation (according to organizational institutions) and external mechanisms of interaction (such as markets) wherein the analogue of our natural environment is nothing but the human (body and soul). This schema of understanding inequality naturally explains the emergence of attempts to transgress humanity to antipodal banks of civilization, such as *anarchy and communism* (that blatantly failed owing to reasons our organizational theory explains), but also suggests scientific principles and mechanisms by which to correct inequality (we propose and analyze in the sequel).

1.1.4 Emotions as Externalities in the Professional Environment

To a large extent, the philosophical and moral basis of Western civilization is, in fact, grounded on the tenet that in professional environments *even emotions are externalities*. This tenet is permeant in social organization to the extent that Western philosophy's dictum that decision-making should be rid of emotional content is one many political and business leaders abide by. In one of the most deleterious practical applications of this tenet, pharmaceutical therapies for psychopathological symptoms are treated with medication meant to induce *cognitive suppression*. I have suffered (and continue to suffer) from such despicable medical practices myself. I continue writing this book under the maxim: Enough is enough! We base our theory of organization on the tenet that emotional content deserves respect and that, in fact, organizational actors should be heartened to let their emotions thrive. In this and the next chapter, we discuss the lack of managing emotional content (other than a stimulus for emotional suppression) as a liability of our organizational faculty.

1.1.5 Understanding and Supplanting Parochial Hierarchical Organization

The preceding discussion suggests that organization suffers from being conducted around tenets that give rise to dysfunctional conditions having negative effects on our well-being and inducing even psychopathological damage to organizational actors. In this monograph, we theorize that the dominant factor contributing to the manifestation of such negative externalities (in the sense of "organizational pollution" affecting the employees of corporations and state organizations) is that organization is fashioned according to hierarchical structures that favor a very limited number of actors at the senior ranks and crowd out a majority of employees from meaningful contribution to organization output. But hierarchical organization damages employees in all ranks not only those at the bottom but also those at the top. Looking into related research in the psychopathology of organization, Langner et al. (2012) show a relationship between social hierarchies and depressive symptoms that manifest in relation to negative emotion suppression to avoid conflict. Blaug (2014) shows that hierarchical organization has a substantially negative effect even at the high ranks due to mechanisms involving the corrupting effect of unrestricted power. We, thus, believe that, in contrast to what is generally believed, the dominant factor in the phenomenon of organizational pollution is not profit maximization (but we do not eliminate the possibility that organizations also need to counteract other factors beyond organizational pollution such as negative environmental impact). In the sequel, we continue to analyze hierarchical organizations for the benefit of understanding what is at stake.

1.2 MOTIVATION: THE DESIGN OF A PUBLIC ADMINISTRATION SYSTEM FOR GREECE

The financial crisis in the United States circa 2008, in "rippling across the Atlantic," instigated a disturbance in the creditworthiness of the Greek state, which provoked a financial and institutional crisis in Greece, a sovereign state and member of the Eurozone, that involves a complex of "organizational morphisms" residing in European Union's young institutional establishment.

These morphisms emerged by virtue of this crisis outside of the scope of the centrally planned European institutions and their legitimacy has troubled theoreticians (e.g., legal theorists) and practitioners (e.g., political leaders) alike. Such spontaneous (political) formations instigate social dynamics (akin to the financial dynamics that threatened the US economy) that threaten the survival of the Greek people, the stability of the emerging notion of a European identity, and, over a longer time span, the survival of human civilization at large.

These observations motivate my thinking in this book: I stipulate that the bedrock of the ongoing crisis can only be prolifically understood through an intellectual framework broader than that concerned with the study of markets, financial institutions, and fiscal policies, in particular, through *organization theory* and *institutional design*. But do not expect there are "textbook recommendations" on how to address the aforementioned threats.

The motivation that drives my intellectual effort in this book concerns the design of a public administration system according to the principles of Greek thought as that manifests in public political debate in Greece and elsewhere (concerning Greece and the European Union at large). In my opinion, the essence of this debate is captured by a notion of *meritocracy* in the sense that the management of public affairs, whether in the running of political institutions or in public administration per se, should be entrusted to the *worthy*. Although the definition of *worth* of a public official is often left unspecified in the colloquial notion of meritocracy, the significance of this concept for Greek culture (as it manifests in public dialogue) cannot be overstated and, in fact, has arguably remained extant throughout the history of the Greeks since ancient times.

In investigating the design of a meritocratic public sector, I have come to believe that the notion of *merit* is not a first order principle around which the organization of the public sector ought to be based on. Nevertheless, the principles I lay out for theorizing about organization are deeply imbued in *Greek thought:* As a student in (Greek) high school I became acquainted with the fundamental principle of organization of the Greek nation, namely, that as

I understood and remember this principle, Greece serves the Greeks rather than the other way round. But how is this possible?

1.3 OUR CONTRIBUTIONS

In this monograph, our contribution is a mathematical theory of organization wherein the individual actor is a first order principal of organization (and organizations are meant to serve these principals). To that end, we draw on a conceptual separation between *organizational actors* (the members of an organization) and *organizational roles* (capacities under which actors contribute to organizational output). Computational perspectives on organization and the theory of algorithms are central to render this separation meaningful and effective. We believe this is the first academic work to analyze the foundations of organization from a computational perspective.

Coming back to the question that motivated this book, we do not attempt to design a public administration system tailored to the specific needs of any manifestation of state organization whether in Greece, in Europe, or elsewhere. Instead, we think from first principles how to structure efforts of designing organizations. In this vein, we make several detailed contributions.

1.3.1 An Analysis of Hierarchical Organization and Delegation

Hierarchies exacerbate the flaws in the institutional foundation of organizations, for example, in subduing every but the highest ranked individual to an upper administrative echelon that alienates the lower echelons of actors. Furthermore, hierarchies create an antagonistic collegiate environment in promoting a struggle to secure high-ranked prominent positions. There exists a rich literature on the perils of hierarchical organization. Our perspective in this monograph is one related to *errors* and *fault tolerance:* Hierarchical architectures based on delegation chains give rise to *single points of failure* in organizational function. We argue that positioning infallible individuals at the root of hierarchies is a futile pursuit as an infallible human nature falls beyond our present grasp.

1.3.2 The Design of Organizations Based on Accountably Anonymous Delegation

We design two organizational institutions based on a primitive we call *accountably anonymous delegation*. In one system, delegation is performed by an *online learning algorithm* and, in the other delegation can be organized in a democratic fashion based on algorithms for matching the role preferences of organizational actors with anonymous evaluations by peers and experts.

1.4 THE INCANDESCENT LIGHT OF THE ORDERS OF REASON

In this monograph, I take the opportunity to address the West from a philosophical perspective in the light of Greece as that resonates in me. To that end, I try to distance myself from Western culture, a process that is certainly facilitated by the fact that Greece has maintained a spiritual orientation independent of that of the West.

To address the West, I feel it is important to appeal to the West's ecclesiastical tradition. That I should consider the religious origins of Western culture occurred to me in virtue of viewpoints and critical thinking expressed in public dialogue by Rev. Nikolaos Loudovikos.[1] He mentions, in particular, that the West's ecclesiastical tradition has had a deep influence on Western philosophy, a viewpoint that both puzzled and captivated me. What was puzzling is that dogmatic faith should interfere with pure reason. But I convinced myself this is a viewpoint I should seriously investigate in recalling related passages from John W. O'Malley's *Four Cultures of the West*.

With this background in mind, my argument is *technical* in the sense of pursuing truth by pure reason. The line of my discourse is paradigmatic of what I consider *good* philosophy in the sense of being useful to science. Unfortunately, philosophy has taken a course independent of science, which many others also acknowledge and similarly criticize. I should remind that science grew out of philosophy and, therefore, that being good to science is something philosophy ought to take responsibility for is not my idea.

Beyond the previous accounts, my motivation for taking on this topic draws on a figure that had haunted me at the Κατεχακη and Μεσογειων traffic light (near the campus of the National Technical University of Athens) I was driving through as an undergraduate student in Athens. There was an elderly but

---

1 See: https://www.youtube.com/watch?v=yuQOa2h87oM.

vibrant man selling sesame bagels (κουλουρια) with a sense of tragic enthusiasm that was reminiscent of my father's enthusiasm in buying lottery tickets. I had taken it up as a responsibility back then to use my best effort to do something about this. Should I feel content that my ethical obligation toward that man trying to make a living in that traffic light against hardship has been fulfilled with this book? I hope that time will tell.

1.4.1 Overview of the Rest of This Book

Chapter 2 is about the cognitive foundation that serves as a basis for organization (and further discusses the duality between the cognitive dimensions of emotion and reason). Chapter 3 poses design requirements and principles organizations should strive to satisfy. Chapter 4 discusses the limitations of hierarchical organization. The elements of our algorithmic theory of governance are presented in Chapter 5 wherein we also present specific designs of organizational systems. We conclude this book in Chapter 6 and further discuss open problems.

2

ON THE COGNITIVE FOUNDATION OF ORGANIZATION

In this chapter, we discuss, starting with Turing machines, computational aspects of cognition and how they relate to our organizational faculty (that is, our ability to join forces in forming organizations). In this monograph, we model organization as a computational problem drawing on the distributed systems paradigm. In this chapter, we further draw a relationship between reason and emotions.

2.1 A MODEL OF COMPUTATION AND THE SYNTHESIS OF PRODUCTS

The standard mathematical model of computation computer scientists use is the *Turing machine*. This is a theoretical model of a computer consisting of an infinite tape with distinct positions (one after the other) for carrying bits and a finite state automaton for controlling a needle having access to the tape that can move left or right and also write elements on the tape as it moves. I will not go into the details of explaining this model: An excellent account of the Turing machine especially for nontheorists is (Pinker, 1997, Chapter 2) and as for theorists I prefer (Goldreich, 2008).

Views that every computation is synthesis and every synthesis is computation are prolific to have in mind throughout this book. Every synthesis (composition) is a computational problem, for can anything (new) emerge without computation? A synthesis proceeds through building new elements from elementary ones, and judging by the etymology, it does so through changes in their relative position. Similarly, a Turing machine proceeds to solve a computational problem transforming elementary data (found on the tape) into sophisticated versions thereof (such as a taking a graph representation as input and giving a *maximal clique* as output). That a Turing machine is a transformation of data follows from the model: at the onset of the computational task input data reside on the tape and that is also where the answer to the problem having been solved resides.

Note it may well be that synthesis is tantamount to computation: The Church-Turing thesis suggests that any computation that can be performed can be performed by a Turing machine. But let me say upfront I believe the Turing machine is not tantamount to computation; however, finding syntheses that cannot be computed by a Turing machine is a challenging pursuit.

Viewing analytical work in mathematics (such as theorem proving), engineering design, and artistic ventures as creative processes of synthesis is something natural but viewing them as computational processes (as I argue above) is perhaps controversial. In my opinion, the reason has to do with the fact that the theory of computation is at an early stage of its development. For example, computability theory is guided by the aforementioned Church-Turing thesis (which I believe is false). To that end, let me ponder: Isn't a theorem whose proof emerges from elementary lemmas, the theorems/results of others, and the rules of logic a computation? That is, has our theorem been computed by the mathematician who proved it? The answer is evidently affirmative to me, but I am not sure about the extent a typical reader would agree. I put forth the perspective thought that understanding computation as the mathematics of synthesis is bound to lead to new analytical perspectives on how to synthesize mathematical proofs, engineering designs, and artistic creations.

2.2 COGNITION AND COMPUTATION

In this monograph, I model the mind using computational models to study organization. That functions of the mind admit computational models is quite well-known in psychology: *Cognitive psychology* and *neuroscience* are disciplines concerned with computation in the mind. In this section, I discuss nonstandard issues in elementary computation that are central to this book's story.

2.2.1 Computability Theory and the Judicial Function of the State

Whether there are limits to computation is a question we are unlikely to find an answer to any time soon. But there are certainly limits to computation using the Turing machine: Turing proved that the HALTING problem, that is, the problem of determining whether a computer program will terminate or will continue to run forever, is *undecidable* using a Turing machine in that there is no Turing machine that can be built to solve the HALTING problem. This result has important implications for the problem of finding *software bugs*, that is, errors in the implementation of software programs – this problem is similarly undecidable. Let us explore a wide-ranging practical implication of this result in social organization and the judicial function in particular.

Let us provide basic background on decision-making first to illustrate the structure the judicial function is based on. We break down the process for a group of parties to reach a decision, say to choose an alternative among a set thereof, into two steps, namely, a *deliberation mechanism* and a *commitment mechanism*. Deliberation explores the consequences of choosing each alternative and how preferable alternatives are to each member of the group. Ideally, if there is no uncertainty in the outcomes, a complete picture emerges out of the deliberation phase and one can, say, apply standard *social choice theory* to make a decision. Otherwise one must factor uncertainty either to extend deliberation into resolving the uncertainty with analytical work or otherwise employ probabilistic models of the world and gauge alternative choices according to their expected benefits. The second step of reaching a decision is a commitment mechanism that commits all members of the group to a particular alternative among the set of options. We point out that this process can be highly tricky even if the decision is *binary*, say, *yes/no*, with the *Byzantine generals problem* serving as an excellent example of how complicated the process of committing to a decision can be.

The system of justice is administratively an organization that is an essential part of the state (much like law enforcement) and whose mission is to produce a good (public) information involving the punishment of unlawful deeds. We may view each trial as an organizational task whose goal is to produce a decision (verdict) on a case involving a (legal) hypothesis about such an unlawful deed (typically, if a person is guilty or not guilty, but trials may even apply to other entities such as organizations or even to entities of institutional character such as laws – for example, there are trials whose goal is to decide whether a piece of regulation is constitutional or not).

The most essential part of a trial is, thus, a *decision*. This decision is, for example, one that involves a possible penalty against a defendant (corresponding to an individual in this case) and the mechanisms by which these decisions are made fall squarely in the framework we have used to structure collective decision-making: A trial is a *collective* decision-making process involving one or more judges (for example, in the US Supreme Court there are seven), a jury, defense attorneys, and others all of whom deliberate before a commitment is made by the judge(s).

A natural question is whether we can use analytical (and mathematical) work in the interest of improving our judgments. I believe the answer is positive: There are techniques to improve the accuracy of our judgments but perfect accuracy is in all likelihood, for the foreseeable future, elusive. Our computational perspective on organizational tasks illuminates the previous statement.

The judicial process is a computational task (of evaluating events). Under the simplifying assumption that humans can be approximated by Turing machines in the execution of the judicial process, then under the HALTING theorem, it is impossible to devise a judicial process that always executes trials correctly without procedural errors. That there are, in fact, many errors that negatively affect judicial decisions is evidenced by the efforts of Ronald Sullivan.[1] In my opinion, the judicial system would greatly benefit by debugging efforts such as those Sullivan pursues in the interest of helping fellow citizens who have been erroneously convicted by procedural errors.

2.2.2 Emersions and Creativity

There is one place Greeks turn to as they try to make important decisions in life (that is, as they contemplate their intimate relationships) and that is nowhere but near the sea.[2]

I was in Eretria (where my country house is) sitting on a pier on the seaside (in my late teens as I was about to become 19), long after midnight, peering at the reflection of the moon on the mild backwash in the form of a figure eight. As my friend approached me, I invited her to do the same. I recall trying to explain the rationale of peering at lunar reflections as the extent to which such *skole* should be worthwhile was not obvious. But shortly, after she asked me to stand up to see what was a glimmering pad of sea reflecting a wide palette of

---

1 See: https://www.youtube.com/watch?v=1fNt95vAQNY.
2 This is appositely captured by Nikos Portokaloglou here: https://www.youtube.com/watch?v=CdZK6TA-ylA.

colors, a phenomenon it was not clear is feasible. We, thus, attributed the phenomenon to fairies and went on with our relationship.

Evi and I promised to keep this our own secret, a promise I broke after discovering how the fairies came to be. The pad where the light was glimmering was next to a small island near the seashore (we were standing on). What I noticed a few years later is that there is a reef in the same location where the glimmering pad was. As the level of the water surface is not constant relative to the reef since there are tides in the area, we had only witnessed a unique way the moon was reflecting on that reef (rather than the reflection of our own spirituality, for example).

That spirituality can reflect in the imagination is clear, but the mechanism is not: I vividly recall to this moment an apparition propping up in my imagination and gently hovering the edge of my balcony in Eretria as Evi told me later that her grandmother had died.

Evi's grandmother was Russian. I would like to draw on this association further:

In conversation with my friend and coworker, Petr Kuznetsov, in Berlin we were pondering the cognitive schemas by which we understand and perceive the pursuit of truth and the emergence of ideas. I recounted two dominant schemas from my own experience, namely, perspectives that emerge as someone assumes a position atop a problem and looking down and another by which an idea emerges in the shape of a sphere from the depths of the sea. The nature of such emersion (viewed from the vantage point of the surface) gives me goosebumps as I think about it. Petr recounted instead viewing truth explorations as operations of digging in the ground. His perspective had never occurred to me (barring reinforcing a verse *I should dig deeper* to myself on negative results from conference submissions) but it was a dominant pattern in my recent work I discussed earlier.

Petr had mentioned another point in a different context that is also worth capturing here: He had shared a thought that there are only so few ideas *around*, that is, in our civilization at large. That point had struck a chord in me as it was highly reminiscent of related conversations (in high school) with Lefteris Tzanoudakis. He had claimed that the global perspective Aristotle had on knowledge is impossible today but in a fashion implying the opposite. Was he wrong?

Errors are important to the thread of this monograph: The undecidability of the HALTING problem suggests that unless the Church-Turing thesis is false, they an inexorable element of human projects. It is by pondering the opposite or inverse of an error I run across an important concept, as important as that of error I believe, namely, that of *emersion*. Emersions are (error prone) constructs that build structure toward the solution of a problem. Viewing organizations as problem-solving enterprises, it is the emersions of organizational actors that drive organizational effort toward success, as it is emersions that make progress toward a mathematical proof, the construction of an engineering device, or the crafting and ultimate production of a music video. The concept of an emersion sticks out as something obvious once the duality between mind and matter has been set into place.

Think of emersions as objects (constructs) of thought rendered by creativity. What do they look like? I tend to think of (creative) emersions as what computer scientists think of as data structures (but I do not think of emersions as being restricted to the discrete form of data structures we know) as well as conjectures that, for example, guide me on how I should proceed with a mathematical proof. I should say that with the concept of an emersion, I try to capture what formed in the mind of Archimedes as he exclaimed *eureka!* What is colloquially referred to as an *eureka moment* is meant to capture the instance an emersion emerges rather than the concept of an emersion per se.

What drives (creative) emersions though? I think we don't know. It is even unclear whether we have a (standard) word for the concept I am discussing here – a "eureka moment" certainly doesn't qualify. That language is the main driver in forming thoughts as objects of cognition is a theory whose plausibility has led scholars to question the extent to which thoughts entailing concepts which we don't have words for can form. False as that sounds, it is certainly the case language facilitates thought clarity. In my opinion, once we think of creativity as an emersion-producing cognitive function, and study the machinery of creativity from such perspective, great progress is bound to take place in this conspicuously opaque area of psychology and cognitive science.

An example of an emersion is a *lyricism*. The term derives from the word $\lambda\upsilon\rho\alpha$, which is a musical instrument the Greeks used since ancient times (a version of which is still in use). I like to write poems and as I read them out loud, others (especially non-Greeks) marvel at my lyricisms. Often to my surprise: What others identify as poetic manifestations of relationships between ideas, they are not but relationships I normally use to understand daily activities. In my opinion, poetic lyricisms emerge naturally in Greeks owing to our close relationship with dualities that emerge at the seashore. In a recent reading of poems by philhellenes at the Hellenic Studies Center of Princeton University in Athens, many of these poems were about the Greek landscape. I think I discerned a process of emersion of lyricisms as the poets started becoming familiar with our landscape.

2.3 ARE REASON AND EMOTIONS DUALS?

Let me proceed to discuss mathematics as a common denominator between ideas and matter. It is perhaps not a coincidence that Freeman Dyson, an important mathematical physicist of celebrated contributions in mathematics and science, has openly stood for dualism between soma and psyche in public debate.[3] In the express conversation, Dyson refers to a quote of Einstein interpreting it as an expression (instance) of a general principle (arguably of religious flavor) that humans cannot understand the psyche and mentality (at least on par with the level of understanding we seem to be capable of attaining with respect to matter and, by extension, the soma). The quote reads as follows: "I see a clock, but I cannot envision the clockmaker. The human mind is unable to conceive of the four dimensions, so how can it conceive of a God, before whom a thousand years and a thousand dimensions are as one?" Dyson does not endorse Einstein's perspective, however.

2.3.1 Mathematical Duality

Quite the contrary, duality principles are blessings in mathematics and physics as they enable the study of phenomena from different perspectives in the interest of drawing complementary conclusions (without much extra analytical work). Dyson acknowledges our limitations in the understanding of the psyche and he seems to suggest that the venture of understanding, for example, consciousness is, in principle, feasible: In my opinion, his remark is suggestive that in virtue of a light of duality between ideas and matter, we can leverage our deep study of matter to understand the opaque at present mathematical universe of the psyche (and consciousness, in particular).

One of the main concerns of mathematical duality are problems of *optimization* where the goal is to optimize an *objective function* subject to *inequality constraints*. That *linear programming* (a version of optimization whereby the objective function is linear and the constraints are linear inequalities) was invented by von Neumann "on the fly" in a meeting with George Dantzig as the latter was discussing with von Neumann his *simplex method,* an algorithm for solving linear programs. Professor Robert Vanderbei mentioned in his course on *optimization* at Princeton that von Neumann's idea must have been influenced by his work on *zero-sum games,* that is, two-players games where each player acts in strict competition with the other in that one

---

3 https://www.youtube.com/watch?v=wxRpa-PqUfw.

player's payoff is the other player's loss. Indeed that zero sum games admit a formulation as linear programs was later formally shown by Albert Tucker.

To render a better understanding of mathematical duality, I need to remark that a duality transformation is a change of perspective of looking at the same object and has a similar effect to that of a mirror: The mirror takes an object and returns a transformed version of the object on the mirror's surface. The original object and that depicted on the mirror are related to one another: Given either object we can identify the other by a transformation.

For example, a duality transformation in mathematical optimization takes as input an optimization problem and returns as output a second optimization problem (the dual) such that the dual of the dual is the original (primal) problem. In a sense, duality is a generalization of the well-known in mathematics notion of an *inverse*. Given an algebraic field, the inverse is a unary operator such that the inverse of the inverse of an element e is again e. In mathematical duality, we are not concerned with fields but rather elements are, for example, optimization problems. Note that as we apply a duality transformation the dual object is not identical: The information content rendered by a transformation in general changes (see below).

2.3.2 Mathematics as Evidence of a Duality Between Matter and Ideas

> *I am afraid that humans are at a turning point of speciation – what is speciation? Lack of reproductive capability between divergent species? I am not sure – maybe speciation has already happened because some humans are already incompatible. What is the relationship between the physical and the mental? Are the spirit and the matter dual concepts? Are natural laws an interface of our minds to communicate through matter or the mind emerges from matter? Is matter an innovation? Why do drugs cure mental diseases? And can mental invocations cure cancer?*
> –Myself in an email to H. Kobayashi (6/29/16)

There is a distinction between matter and ideas that has a philosophical bearing in the distinction between *materialism* and *idealism*. There is an expressed philosophical perspective that these philosophical theories are dual perspectives of looking at the cosmos. The question of the extent to which ideas and matter are related does not have a clear answer. My perspective, and the thesis I postulate in this monograph, is that this relationship is strong: A surprising fact that scientists often run into in their study of nature is that natural phenomena more often than not admit explanations using theories formulated in the language of mathematics. In fact, even mathematical imagination has a bearing in science as mathematical work developed outside the purview of nature often ends up finding scientific applications especially in physics.

I believe that the duality between ideas and matter, as that is expressed in philosophy, can assume a mathematical formalization in that there exists a *mathematical transformation* that can help us navigate between idealistic and materialistic perspectives of looking at the cosmos in a precise fashion. But ideas and matter are *not* always equal ways of the looking at an object, a principle that is captured under the term *parity violation* in mathematical physics.

The term *parity violation* is standard in physics: *Parity transformations* are mathematical transformations that operate on quantum mechanical systems (involving particles) giving new quantum-mechanical systems. Parity violation manifests when the information content of a system and the information content of a related system obtained under a parity transformation are different. Duality transformations have an analogous property: The dual of an optimization problem can, for example, be easier to solve than the respective primal. Primal, dual, and primal/dual algorithms for solving optimization problems can deviate substantially operating on principles exploiting different properties of the respective (primal/dual) structures.

Parity violation can be especially helpful in applications of mathematical duality in medicine: We are going to explore duality as a method of reasoning about the soma and the psyche as dual pairs. In this context, parity violation implies that we can use somatic mechanisms (such as pharmaceutical drugs) to cure mental diseases and psychotherapeutic treatment for somatic diseases (such as cancer). In fact, the prescription of pharmaceutical drugs is standard for the treatment of psychiatric conditions. Furthermore, it used to be a common medical practice to transfer patients to locations with favorable climatic conditions as treatment for somatic disease.

2.3.3 Mathematics Evince a Duality Between Reason and Emotions

Drawing on the aforementioned relationship between the soma and the psyche, I would like to make a case that a relationship exists between reason and emotions (one that couples them under a transformation). To that end, note that the main components of our psyche are, at an empirical level, reason on one hand and emotions on the other. Since emotions involve a somatic experience (beyond the somatic experience we understand using our cognition and brain), mathematical work (a predominantly cognitive experience) having an impact on our soma would imply the existence of a relationship between reason and emotions. But this is certainly familiar to anyone who has tried out carrying out mathematical work. Doing mathematics can be a painful experience, for example, through the stress it exerts on our soma. I discuss issues of this nature further in this book, but I need to mention that should we be able to understand the physical/somatic stress that mathematics brings about, we could facilitate teaching mathematics to those that resist the effort and underperform on this subject owing to the somatic and emotional stress that is brought about. I believe that reason and emotions are, in fact, dual pairs in a mathematical sense.

There are also other ways through which a relationship between reason and emotions can be inferred from a mathematical lens: Mathematical ventures, whether ones of basic (pure) research or ones having to do with the applications of mathematics in modeling physical phenomena and with engineering applications, arguably have a strong component of *risk* in the sense that once that you set out on a mathematical venture it is highly unclear whether and to what degree the venture will be successful. This is especially true as the level of abstraction is raised, an observation my high school mathematics instructor, Georgios Chalapas, had brought to my attention early on. I wasn't sure what he meant. Frankly, I can only empirically understand his point even now.

Chalapas instilled to me through mathematics a rigor in thinking no other subject or teacher has managed to to this point whether during my formal education or during the friction I've had with mathematics (or other related subjects) through self-study and research. I feel as if I know the reason: I used to marvel as a student with the blackboards he was painting equations on – I had even pointed out at the end of one class that he should take a picture of the blackboard he was about to erase because it would have been a pity for the blackboard's content to fall into oblivion. I can still remember his humble reaction and sense of pride he showed in receiving my compliment.

But how does this relate to risk? Toward drawing a relationship between risk and aesthetic perspectives, consider an actor and a task the actor is pondering whether to take up. Certainly the task's mental representation in the actor's mind factors in as an essential, if not the most important, element in his effort to decide – although the monetary reimbursement typically associated with decisions of this nature could certainly factor as important in the actor's decision effort as well, I only want to consider the implications the salary has on his or her perceived ability to perform the task rather than external to the task factors such as the quality of wine he or she can afford by virtue of the salary.

In this mental representation, there are aspects in the task's projected execution that are unclear. Let us consider these aspects as "details" that need to be sorted out in order to make a decision. Introspecting on the effort that is required to fill in those details and to what extent our decision-maker believes he or she will be able to successfully perform the tasks is indisputably the decisive aspect of the decision as we have framed it. Our thought experiment thus reduces the concept of risk to the cognitive processes involved in our actor's drifting mind. Certainly, the extent to which this mental simulation is aesthetically pleasing to the actor is rather critical on the decision outcome.

Let me give an example from courtship rituals. My favorite decision to ponder in life is whether and how to approach a female being in all of her grandeur as her resonating presence affects her environment including me of course. I have naturally pondered this question a lot and I have reached the conclusion that how a presence resonates in me can be different from how that presence resonates in others around me. This phenomenon begs the question what the principles that underly my observation are. That a scientific explanation exists is plausible: Cognitive science suggests something as imperceptible as *pupil dilation* in a glance can serve as an intimation of feelings of affinity.

That the relationship between a visual perspective and algebra can be made precise is clear to anyone having proven a theorem whose formulation was influenced by geometric thinking. That an aesthetic perspective can be translated to algebra, ample evidence lies in the manifestation of the *golden ratio* in art and architecture. That an aesthetic perspective that be related to science evidence lies in the *Fibonacci sequence*, a sequence whose elements can be derived from a formula that uses the golden ratio, a sequence that models a variety of evolutionary phenomena. All in all, I have argued that the emotional content of an aesthetic perspective can be used on par in decision-making with the rigorous approach of mathematical reasoning. That some of us prefer one approach to make decisions while others prefer the other can only be taken as evidence that a relationship between the approaches exists. How to make this relationship rigorous beyond the golden ratio is an interesting question for future work.

2.4 CHANGING PERSPECTIVES AS A COMPUTATIONAL PRIMITIVE

We are accustomed to quantifying *risk* with *probabilities*. But the extent to which this model is meaningful as a means of reasoning about (organizational or other) tasks (for example, in the interest of making decisions) depends on the nature of the task and our objective. Certainly, decisions that involve uncertainty can be informed by means other than, for example, assigning probabilities to possible states of nature to derive the expected utility of alternatives in order to choose the alternative that maximizes expected utility: Decisions informed by the subjective measure of how aesthetically pleasing an alternative appears to the decision-maker can make more sense, depending of course on the decision maker's profile and buildout. What's more by mathematically exploring the extent to which these perspectives can be made consistent can lead to important discoveries (such as the Nash equilibrium and its existence principle) shedding light on human nature and evolution.[4]

Changes in perspective are useful from navigating a territory to solving mathematical equations to building organizational infrastructure. Navigating in unfamiliar territory, say, a city, is a frequently useful computational task. To get from a starting location to a destination instructions based on traffic signs and landmarks could do but alternatively a coordinate tracking system coupled with a map could make the navigational task a lot easier. The latter possibility typically requires a satellite constellation to track present location as in the Global Positioning System (GPS). The principle we are illustrating is no other than the simple observation that a *change in perspective* can make life easier. But also that, such changes in perspective are not necessarily easy to accomplish. With respect to solving equations, the Fourier and Laplace transforms transform certain difficult to analyze differential equations to simple algebraic equations (whose solutions are easy to obtain and transform back to the original domain).

Changes in perspective are easy to ponder from a duality perspective: The duals of a *convex optimization problem* are different, even distinctly so,[5] but equivalent (for the purpose of obtaining the optimal solution/answer) ways of looking at a problem. In linear and convex optimization theory, there are algorithmic approaches to obtaining optimal answers that work solely with the primal or dual (respectively) formulations but there are also many

---

[4] See: https://www.youtube.com/watch?v=LJS7Igvk6ZM.

[5] For example, in applications of optimization to the design of computer networks, duality transformations are important in network function decompositions for the benefit of obtaining distributed implementations of a network design (Chiang et al., 2007).

algorithms (called *primal-dual algorithms*) that simultaneously work on both perspectives (for the benefit of obtaining an optimal solution).

With respect to organizational infrastructure, working in teams can be more effective in attaining corporate goals rather than playing solitaire. Especially in hierarchical relationships, developing affinity for your supervisor/manager/boss certainly facilitates a better understanding of his or her perspective (putting yourself in his or her shoes) on how to conform to corporate and (certainly) group management policies as you work toward the attainment of your professional and corporate goals. In personal communication with Professor Hisashi Kobayashi (my PhD thesis advisor at Princeton), he mentioned that the Japanese tend to express a sense of respect for those in superior places in corporate (professional) hierarchies that often comes from the heart.

An important element of our theory of organization is a separation between *organizational actors* and *organization roles*. Assuming a different role facilitates a change in perspective in an organization. The *Stanford prison experiment* suggests that roles can have a transformative effect on the corresponding actors (even in experimental settings). Our architecture for structuring organizations facilitates such transformations while being cautious to avoid a negative impact on the actors through creating role boundaries: Organizations become responsible for administratively (for example, through software interfaces) separating roles. Organizations are also responsible for enabling actors to take a distance from the roles they assume through providing emotional content necessary to make roles productive without incurring emotional externalities to the respective actors.

Perspectives are an important topic of discussion in Chapter 4.

3

ORGANIZATIONAL SYSTEMS DESIGN REQUIREMENTS

3.1 WHAT MOTIVATES EFFORT AND PERFORMANCE

Let us look first into motivational aspects of organization. Our argument is organized around the idea that it takes *motivation* to mobilize *effort*. Let us thus look into motivation in more detail. Of course what we are interested in is motivation to perform in organizational tasks, for example, under capacities in the public sector or the corporate (business) world. Thus motivation for economic performance is certainly within our purview. But this is not a good place to start in discussing motivation as the vast majority of the Western population is generally displeased with their professional capacities and tasks they face within such roles. To solely rely on these pessimistic views in the interest of exploring motivation from first principles, we would be faced with risk of systemic bias in our conclusions.

Instead, we turn our attention to human relationships based on *erotic intimacy*. That erotic intimacy can mobilize effort is a simple fact for any Greek. As a student in high school, my motivation to study hard for the exams leading to the opportunity for university education was my desire to have the opportunity to entertain and be entertained by a female company elegant in sophistication. My instructor in the subject of composing essays, namely, Lefteris Tzanoudakis, who used to drive me to his office on Saturday mornings, an opportunity for company we both took advantage of for the benefit of entering engaging conversations, had been cautious enough to warn me about the obstacles I would face in pursuing the company of attractive females without good university education. Being Greek, the Trojan War was fought for beautiful Helen after all.

Looking out for one's passion is often rewarding whether in professional or personal matters. Esther Perel discusses in an enlightening talk[1] that looking out for one's passion beyond a committed relationship is something we often do even if that jeopardizes our emotional security. She explores affairs as acts of infidelity to our committed partners (going beyond romantic ideals of commitments) that are able to fulfill anything one could ask for in a romantic relationship. She goes on say that affairs serve as antidotes to death, that they are more about desire than they are about sex, and that the drivers to pursue affairs involve desire for novelty, for attention, and a desire to feel special and important. I use her perspective to calibrate motivation in professional matters.

Why should the qualities anyone should look out for in their professional passions be any different than those that Esther Perel identifies in her account of erotic intimacy? Shouldn't work be an antidote to death and a pursuit for the eternal (rather than the ephemeral that perishes)? Shouldn't we pursue novelty in our professional environment, interesting colleagues who through their perspectives will help us grow our personalities, and challenging projects to work on that will have an impact in our professional environment? Shouldn't we get the attention of our colleagues as we contribute to those projects ideas and their development, and shouldn't we expect to feel special and important if our work goes well adding value to our professional environment?

3.2 PRODUCTIVITY AS A DRIVER OF ORGANIZATIONAL EFFORT

We stipulate that individuals have a natural propensity for impact on their respective organizations. Organizations should build on that propensity and motivate their members to pursue productive impact. We, thus, arrive at our first design requirement in building organizational systems:

Every actor should be given the opportunity to pursue productive impact on his or her organization.

In fact, organizations should take a step further to employ means of aligning the incentives of their members so that as these actors join forces they increase the value of the productive impact being affected. Organizations should, thus, look for and reap coordination opportunities among their corresponding actors. In this vein, let me present a simple but interesting

---

1 See her TED talk on "Rethinking infidelity ... a talk for anyone who has ever loved."

institutional mechanism to motivate actors to organize around ambitious projects in a fashion that manages an elementary risk entailed in the stability of sustaining challenging ventures, namely, that actors have an incentive to flee for the benefit of pursuing alternative low-in-risk but safer in the payoffs undertakes.

Consider a two-player stag hunt: Each player has two strategies, namely, either to cooperate in hunting stag or independently hunt hare. Of course a stag is better nutrition than a hare. If a player hunts stag and the other doesn't, the former is sure to be unsuccessful in the hunt and since he or she expends energy for the hunt he or she is worse off than having hunted hare alone. Both players hunting stag and both players hunting hare are the only pure strategy equilibria in the game.

Suppose now the hunters make an agreement that "whatever one earns, he or she gives that to the other" (except for sharing the stag) an agreement which can be enforced through a third party (having the authority to enforce commitments). Should the players enter such agreement, neither player has an incentive to hunt hare nor they join each other in hunting stag (The mathematical effect of such an agreement in the payoff structure is that the payoff matrices are transposed and cooperation in hunting stag becomes the unique Nash equilibrium of the game). The effect of the feasibility of such agreements in an organization that supports them is that the members of the organization would tend to focus their efforts on higher risk projects that require cooperation to succeed (Without a centralized party such agreements are hard to enforce). Studying analogous mechanisms as the number of players increases is an interesting question for future work.

3.3 EMOTIONS AS DRIVERS OF ORGANIZATIONAL EFFORT

I previously discussed that purposed existence can lead to negative somatic and cognitive externalities and that human beings should adopt a purpose (be that in professional or personal matters) with great care. For example, if the purpose of marrying is to bear children, then marriage defeats the purpose of a spouse. There is one purpose though in my life I feel comfortable adopting and that is to seek *emotional depth*. I live by the hope I will ever be able to experience refined, complex, and unusual positive emotions. But deeply emotional experiences are elusive without a sharp intellect. Similarly honing your intellectual capacity requires access to robust emotional experiences.

By the previous argument that reason and feelings admit an understanding based on duality transformations (through linking mathematical inquisitiveness and ardor to somatic symptoms [and pain]), I stipulate that the reasoning impact of refined feelings is visible at a conceptual level even to those of us that are not versed in mathematical formalisms and similarly that refined feelings can hone the analytical ability of a mathematician (and even debug errors in mathematical statements and theorems, a notoriously difficult task). The proverb that decisions in organizations should be rid of emotional content (a proverb that has its origins in philosophical debate of past centuries) is, in my opinion, harmful. That is not to say we should compromise rigor with emotionality though.

In fact, I take it as a simple fact that emotionality is at odds with analytical rigor: Emotionality can compromise organizational output (be that a material product or a financial service). In this vein, my thesis in this monograph, a thesis which I pose as fundamental principle of organization, is that organizations should foster the manifestation of robust emotional content among employees.

For example, I believe that mixing business and pleasure should be encouraged. This may be a fine line in organizational protocol. But on the flip side aren't we already walking a fine line in adopting organizational protocol in the pattern of cold Weberian bureaucracies?

That bureaucracies induce negative emotional impact on organizational actors is an indisputable fact. But there are other factors that induce the manifestation of negative emotions: Our economic system is organized such that making a living should rest on summoning financial resources from work. Thus, the fear that access to those resources can be crowded out by competitors (other actors being part of what is usually referred as a *workforce*) leads to a breaking down of our emotional stability and negatively affects our work leading to a vicious cycle of negative performance and negative emotions such as anxiety.

The emotional stress that actors have to go through in their professional matters is not usually addressed within the organizational structures that induce it but it is rather relegated to the medical profession leading to the typical enactment of pharmaceutical treatments by medical doctors who have no control over the factors that create the emotionally harmful behavior. I stipulate that organization should not only take responsibility for the negative emotional content they create among their employees but they should rather assume responsibility for generating emotionally stable professional environments that stimulate creativity.

For as long as organizational actors feel they can muster their creative potential toward meaningful organizational output, the fear of being crowded out by a workforce that is, for example, content with lower pay for posts of standardized performance qualifications vanishes. In contrast, employment that is open ended on the nature of the work an actor can contribute induces different organizational dynamics where anxiety manifests in more prolific varieties: Will I fit in? And how can I leverage the organizational culture toward my advantage in the work I opt to carry out?

In my opinion, the model whereby organizations fix, through their top-level management, their products and services and hire personnel that meet the qualifications top-level management and then hiring personnel believe would fit the materialization of such specific output is wrong. I do not believe that such a practice should be eliminated from the repertoire of hiring strategies even if the ideas I put forth in this book start to pan out, but I believe that hiring behavior should instead be structured according to the principle that organizational actors should have room for distinctively unique contributions according to their agendas for professional growth and skill.

To summarize, we propose that organizations, especially those focused on generating products and services whose materialization requires analytical work, beyond analytically evaluating contributions according to principles of justice based on contribution (see below), ought to be responsible for facilitating the emergence of emotional content (for example, in the organizational culture, but our recommendation goes beyond the behavioral norms that develop to shape employee motivation and collegiate atmosphere) that is conducive to the emergence of creative analytical work. Dubbing this principle *basilica is a right* it corresponds to a shift from rational organization.

The emergence of shared content in a process of emotional synthesis is, thus, a first order desideratum in the theory of organization we propose in this monograph. Many things at stake in collaborative environments related to emotional content are often deemed *nuances* in the sense of being elusive (given current organizational methods). Wired as we are in a mode of thinking around hierarchies we miss out on important opportunities for prolific modes of making decisions that typically manifest outside their confines into teamwork gamuts that are rare and rare enough to evade opportunities for productively shaping the (decision) faculty required to make them prolific.

A typical mode of carrying out academic work is that exemplified in Isaac Newton's style of research in the paradigm of *If I have seen further, it is only by standing on the shoulder of giants*. The paradigm Newton followed in his research was one imbued in the grandeur solitude offers. I had the opportunity to come to my own understanding of his mode of thinking in the Wren library at Trinity College at Cambridge, one I deeply relate to. This paradigm is reflected in the aforementioned maxim. But that is only one mode of collective decision-making characterized by loose coordination among individuals that is worthwhile for organization to take further.

To the end of understanding what can go wrong with collective decision-making in a research collaboration between giants, let me now draw on Murray Gell-Mann's perspective on his collaboration with Richard (Dick) Feynman.[2] Gell-Man reflects on this collaboration with a sense of bitterness owing to a lack of compatibility in the style of engagement: In trying to give his best for the benefit of the output of the collective effort without being attentive to accrediting contribution at the early stages of the collaboration, he had to meet an antithetical style of carrying out research by Dick Feynman who was trying to get credit for his thoughts as they were emerging in conversation.

In my opinion, an important desideratum in organization is the building of *open-ended collaborations*. If the scope of a collaborative effort is a priory approximately fixed, it is possible for a disincentive to emerge that others take up the majority of the work. This phenomenon gives an impetus to top-down organization that delegates work in clearly specified components, which tends, however, to compartmentalize the collegiate atmosphere in strata and departments in a fashion that demotes opportunities for collaboration.

I believe this paradigm of joint cogitation can be taken further using physical means of engagement, for example, in projects that involve combinations of scientific and artistic contributions. Science and art can be understood as complementary perspectives of viewing the same objects of observation in the cosmos, whether nature, life, or human relationships. Scholarly thought would benefit from understanding science and art in this fashion even from a pragmatic perspective. As I was attending a conference organized by the European Commission, in a colloquial conversation with an attendee she discussed an idea of the Commission that European research funding agencies should provision for funding artists in conjunction with scientists in their projects. In my opinion, such initiative has the potential to benefit research at European institutions and elsewhere. I also believe that artists can meaningfully contribute to the synthesis of the emotional content that organizations can leverage in the interest of generating scientific and mathematical output.

---

2 As Gell-Mann reflects on that collaboration here: https://www.youtube.com/watch?v=HNsaTskCYPQ.

3.4 EFFORT SHOULD BE REWARDED ACCORDING TO CONTRIBUTION

Squarely at the heart of this book lies a paradox that corrals organization's first principles as we have been trying to understand them from the perspective of distributed computation. The paradox is the logical disparity between *justice* as an institution of the state and *debugging* as the epitome of software development. What is paradoxical in the side-by-side comparison of these concepts is that although, on one hand, their relevance becomes apparent once we try to align their meanings (and immediately clear in trying to picture Sherlock Holmes investigating an incidence of the infamous blue screen of death of the Windows operating system), on the other, the retributive character of justice is a literary anastrophe of the creative character of software development. The paradox can thus be resolved by atoning justice with a creative mission.

3.4.1 Rational Justice

One way to understand this book is as an argument toward the end of *displacing* rationality in organization from a property the system as a whole should exhibit to a property the individual as an organizational actor should exhibit. In a sense, we propose a shift from the incumbent principle of *rational organization* to one of *rational justice in organization*. Rational organization is exemplified in *Weberian bureaucracies* viewing the individual as *a gear in an apparatus*.

We live in the era of Isaac Newton: Our civilization is based on a paradigm whose maxim is the *rational organization of matter*. Physics, chemistry, biology, engineering, and medicine are at the forefront of science. These disciplines seek ever more refined theories to understand and leverage the material structure of the cosmos. Physics studies the material structure of the universe, chemistry studies molecules, biology seeks to understand the elementary structure of living organisms, engineering seeks to synthesize material artifacts fit for industrial production, and medicine seeks to understand the principles of our soma and develop pharmaceutical treatment of disease.

Organization (be that social or industrial) is no exception: Our daily lives are organized in time blocks of work and entertainment both of which are typically standardized in a socially orderly fashion. We are mustered in *human resources departments* to enter orderly (top-down) organizational structures intended to drive the (industrial) production of goods and services. Those who are reluctant to perform under the psychologically debilitating pressure to serve as a means toward production are relegated to poverty. Scientific knowledge production is no exception to the pattern of standardization and those of us who are fortunate to have excelled in educational pursuits have to compete in *job markets* advertising and selling our (academically pristine) skills as commodities. Entertainment is similarly standardized in television programs, sports events, and the like.

Once this perspective is in place the reasons for the failure of such model as an organizational motif become immediately apparent, e.g., to anyone familiar with Greek culture and the Greek public sector – arguments for other bureaucracies can follow suit. What we propose to replace this with though is not immediately apparent why it makes sense. For example, why do we discuss rational individuals on par with rational justice in the organizations wherein they partake?

I will start with an example from my own professional experience: Professor Jennifer Rexford's arrival at Princeton, in the Computer Science Department, as I was a graduate student in the Electrical Engineering Department, was a turning point, not only in my professional career (as she ended up being in my PhD thesis committee and I ended up being in her group as a postdoctoral researcher after graduation), but also in my life, for an important reason. Prior to our collaboration my work was grappling with a particular kind of strife, namely, as I was working on research papers, in building on my arguments and results and discovering plausible refutations and, more generally, issues that required attention, in discussing such issues with my collaborators (mostly advisors), the typical response was a blunt *don't worry about it*, an argument that merely refutes progress.

Both as an undergraduate student at the National Technical University of Athens and later as a graduate student at Princeton University I was quite competent but also quite anxious. Should I attribute the pacification gestures I had been experiencing as acts of kindness in purportedly gently addressing my anxiety issues? The extent to which I had anxiety issues can be debated. But, in my opinion, the mollification of existential anxiety is problematic for a variety of reasons: (1) Anxiety should not be understood as collateral psychological damage from leading hectic lives (e.g., striving to reach the top of the academic pyramid as graduate students often do) and, although it can be pathological, a more prolific perspective of looking at it is an emotional state that drives us to mobilize our problem-solving abilities to formulate and solve the problems we formulate. (2) Anxiety can also be understood as a driver for a related emotion, namely, *curiosity* in the sense of a driver for exploration – although wonder can certainly drive our curiosity, the universe of ideas does not always present in the most glorious of fashions. (3) Anxiety related to core issues in our existence has a philosophical flavor that should not be dismissed by academics in engineering and mathematics departments as irrelevant. In my opinion, philosophical thinking is a primordial state of rigorous, verifiable scientific discoveries, thus the effect of mollifying existential anxiety is an output of incremental results in defiance of groundbreaking scientific and mathematical work.

Simulations of a *judgment day* had been running amok in my head time and again and, as I have come to realize, these simulations are not mere theoretical curiosities. What was driving me amok as a student concerned issues I faced time and again in the process of my professional growth.

What Jen did differently from other academics I had the opportunity to interact with was to be attentive to the issues I was raising in the course of our research and to be perceptive in how she was responding to these issues. It was a pleasure interacting with her in a variety of ways, for example, through write-ups typically meant to grow into paper submissions but also in email and in especially enjoyable face-to-face conversations. Jen also had a transforming impact on my ability to exhibit composure as I *was taking in feedback* from paper reviews, an ability that was important in our field (computing and networking systems research) where the community places great emphasis on the quality of a paper's write-up as an indicator of whether it should be accepted for publication.

Coming back to my thesis that rational justice is a necessary condition for rationality, I have to quote Aristotle that humans are political animals. We want our ideas and contributions to dialogue to be discussed and appreciated and there is a natural inclination for our cognitive ability to decline if our contribution efforts face dead-ends. In contrast, in rational organization such as in Weberian bureaucracies (that are rigidly hierarchical) the possibilities for dialogue are restricted to the protocol constraint that one should perform as instructed – it is not our ideas that are being evaluated and valued in such systems of organization but how well we do in what has been delegated to us as a responsibility, in most cases, with little attention to our creative potential.

3.4.2 Defensible Arguments: The Aquiline Pupil of Mathematical Rigor

Much of the thinking required to write this monograph started out as I was a senior researcher at Deutsche Telekom Laboratories in Berlin, Germany. I spent most of the time indulging in mathematical pursuits to teach myself mathematics. I built my own syllabi based on mathematical subjects I was finding enjoyable to read. The process was often tedious as it was not clear which books to read and which video lectures to watch (fortunately, many academics had started recording their lectures and uploading them online). One evening as I was hanging out with friends in Berlin, I complained to a (Greek) friend that I find it nearly impossible to read the books that reviews say are accessible to the readership and enjoyable to read those books that reviews mark as advanced and difficult to parse. She gave me a reason for that, one I pondered deeply about: She said that introductory books do not explain the intuition behind a subject giving only the logistics of how things work.

Soon after, I formulated a question capturing the situation I was facing and what the issues at stake were: *Which of the two is more important? How or why?* Let me illustrate the question from the perspective of algorithms and their theory. *How an algorithm works* is important to implement the algorithm and use it in practice. *Why an algorithm works* involves a correctness proof (that the algorithm is indeed correctly computing what it is supposed to in every case) and possibly a related performance analysis (for example, demonstrating that the algorithm has good performance [polynomial with a small leading exponent] as otherwise it would be impractical to implement it).

In my experience with algorithmic problems, it is worth trying to alternate between *how* and *why* in designing an algorithm: The analysis informs the design and pondering the design space enlightens the analysis. The aforementioned (simply stated) question was thus important to me to hone my approach to solving algorithmic problems.

From the perspective of rational justice in organization, an analysis that involves, say, algorithmic work as contribution to organizational output can convince others that the effort is worthwhile. Professional organizations are reluctant to allocate time to employees to carry out a theoretical analysis of their output, an observation that applies even to academic institutions (especially in computer science) in that some committees that evaluate paper submissions for possible publication place little credit to theoretical analyses. In my opinion, numerical and simulation work can only capture a limited aspect of algorithmic and engineering design. It is my humble opinion that professional and academic organizations should place more emphasis on theory and that methods should be explored to incentivize employees to add theory to their standard work schedule.

3.4.3 Rational Justice Is Hard

My deviant perspective on things had been recognized early on by Professor Randy Wang as we had interacted in his graduate course on *advanced operating systems principles* at Princeton. As I acknowledge in my PhD thesis, the subject I took up to work on in my thesis came up in his course, actually shortly before a psychological breakdown, at its onset, that is, of what one could describe as the manic side of an episode of manic depression. That is what the medical team that took over treatment initially thought the nature of my breakdown was. But they retracted from that position a few years later: For example, the opinion of my psychotherapist, Dr Marvin Geller, was that my symptoms were not being triggered by events of somatic (physical) nature.

I still recall the vivid representation in my mind of a major issue that could arise in the scenario I was doing my course project on. I was working on a problem related to routing in wireless networks in ad hoc mode in that the physical topology could be arbitrary and volatile (changing). The project involved using locations (for example, from GPS measurements) to improve routing performance. But what struck me as interesting was what would happen should nodes start maliciously dropping the packets they were meant to forward. There was no way the protocols (algorithms) we had in mind back then could defend against such misbehavior. Randy immediately recognized the significance of the problem I had formulated (that is, how to design algorithms and protocols to defend against malice in routing) and I, thus, changed projects.

In coming back to Princeton after a 1-year Leave of Absence, security had become a hot topic – the 9/11 incident had certainly had great influence to that end. I changed advisors resuming my collaboration with Professor Kobayashi, who encouraged me to work on the security problem I had formulated in Randy's course, and Randy was willing to help me in my effort. Randy and I wrote a paper that is still frequently cited even today. Many aspects in that paper illustrate a variety of points in this chapter.

Let me draw on one experience, in particular, I have time and again recounted to others (at Princeton) as striking. Shortly before the conference (Infocom) deadline I was aiming for to submit my work (performed as it had been in the solitude of my room at the Graduate College), Randy decided to go through my paper to put it in a stylistic format befitting that which was expected by the conference. He did a fantastic job rewriting the paper front to back, nervous as I was tracking his changes. But his effort came to a halt in the last section as he could not understand the point I was making there: "The paper does not fly like this" he wrote in email. I recall attributing to Randy an idea of me as someone who had tried to rush in garbled content (in draft mode) to match the number of pages the conference had set as an upper bound on the length of submissions.

But I did not get mad. What I did instead was to kindly ask him to reread that section as I went on a coffee date at Starbucks with Marcy Block, a beautiful New Yorker doing her PhD in English literature. In coming back to my office, nervous as I had been throughout that date, I found an email from Randy saying he finally understood what I had done and that it was *genius*. In the email, he CC'ed Professor Arvind Krishnamurthy (one of his collaborators at Yale) as (in his own words) evidence of his remarking that my work is genius. I should recount my experience on how I came up with the main idea used in this opaque result: What I recall is a lightning bolt striking me in my dorm room as I thought the problem my algorithm solves indeed admits a solution. But it took a period of few months to transform the idea that this experience imprinted on me into a correct algorithm. It is a bitter disappointment that I have never come across follow-up literature discussing this particular aspect of my paper: I don't think anyone has built on it, and it is highly unclear to what extent anyone has taken the time to understand it, as Randy did.

3.4.4 Rational Justice and Rationalization

Rationalization is, in principle, something positive, namely, an effort to apply principles of rationality to understand decisions. The term *rationalization* can also have a negative connotation as a process of applying rationality principles to hide the true motives in decision-making whether to oneself or others. For example, the term is often used in psychology in the latter negative sense, as negative was the context in which I learned the term in high school, to the extent I remember. Viewing rationalization in a purely negative context is something bad for rational justice: Since a decision, for example, in the context of politics, can in itself be a great contribution (on par with a work of art or a mathematical theorem), emphasizing the negative meaning of rationalization refutes understanding decisions from a rational perspective (against our rational justice principle).

To what extent can rationalization be credible? Let me discuss this question with an example: A paradigm of stock market trading is what is often called *high-speed trading* whereby traders, rather than directly issuing individual trading orders, devise instead algorithms, implemented in software that is executed in computing platforms having direct access to the stock market platform that can issue trading orders at a "wire speed." Let me, thus, rephrase the previous question in this context. To what extent can one understand the trading strategy of a particular trader or trading organization by observing the sequence of trading orders? This question is rather important as it is not unlikely trading agents acting adversarially against the stock market can manifest in the future. I should say, judging from my research experience in security issues on the internet that the answer is hardly easy. For example, ponder: What if malicious trading organizations try to evade detection? I hope I have convinced you the issues at stake are high.

Rationalization is related to the *what if analysis* Steven Covey discusses in his book on the habits of effective people. A grandfather I used to play backgammon with in my early childhood, being on summer vacation at our country house in Eretria, introduced me to a related type of analysis I call *what might have been analysis,* in virtue of Metallica's The Unforgiven,[3] which cannot be more relevant to this book's subject. Actually, this book branched off another book I recently started to write I tentatively call *The Incandescent Light of the Orders of Reason.*

The first chapter begins as follows:

> *Dim as the light of the Selene is, a captivating feeling of awe in pondering the bedrock of the Milky Way cannot humble me but only inspire me to keep looking up unlike my natural thinking schema of always looking down, a schema that consumes me still one more time as I turn a blind eye to the grandeur I am hoping to be called upon to surpass. But that was then and this is now.*
>
> *I posit that retrospective manifestations of reality are meaningful. For example, in writing the previous paragraph I extrapolated my thinking out of a vivid visual memory of the sky in Corfu.*
>
> *I could not see the moon, still it must have existed as it always does. Its light must have been dim enough to unbar the stardom's opulence unlike the categorical austerity of the kingdom of heaven a full moon constricts. Still I have not even started to articulate my purported argument.*
>
> *I am so trying to formulate a convincing argument that to extrapolate a thinking process out of a visual memory is meaningful. For example, we as humans extrapolate thinking processes to the conscious life that surrounds us. I carefully*

---

3 See: https://www.youtube.com/watch?v=Ckom3gf57Yw.

> distinguish the thinking process of conscious life from that of, say, mushrooms if a mushroom can ever be contemplated of as being adroit at thinking.
>
> I can, nevertheless, ever freely ponder whether asking which hue in the palette of a cat's emotional state to use to dye the iced jelly cube my cat sips on as she quenches her thirst from the bowl of refrigerated water I often serve her is more favorable than serving my cat tap-water.
>
> I will refer to the process of extrapolating thinking *from* observable fact *as* attribution. ...

Cat Pierce, an artist I hold in high esteem, was on my mind in writing the previous passage. Goldfrapp's Zodiac Black, from her latest album, certainly befits the mood and served as an inspiration; I cracked the meaning of her song's title in writing that passage. That music evokes colors is something I heard for the first time from a coworker at T-Labs as he mentioned a composer who thought that the light is dimmed in performances so that the colors are more visible.

So *attribution* is something very important and the first topic I pondered as I started to think and write what has come out as this book. In fact, my idea was to model attribution as a *computational phenomenon*. We are certainly a long way from that, or are we not? The first version of this monograph came out in a blizzard of writing effort in thinking the computational foundations of attribution. But of course the background materials I use here have a much longer history.

A mechanism by which stereotypes trigger misjudgment is through triggering *misattribution*, for example, through ascribing a false attribute to an individual in the stereotype's image. But attribution is meant in the previous passage as something more general, namely, as the ability to assume the position of another intellect, say, with reference to a creative work or of your own intellect at another point in time (as I was trying to do above). The extent to which I can assume my own former cognitive state with reference to creative work I have done in the past is highly unclear and, to a large extent, risky. This is well known in psychology under *recursion*.

The extent to which one can assume the position of someone else should, in principle, be as risky as recursion. But, doable as it often is, it can also be a rewarding experience. In fact, this is something I do all the time in reading mathematical proofs: To understand a proof what I try to do is to enter the mind of the *proofmaker* in the interest of understanding his *proof strategy*.

In preparing to discuss attribution here, I looked for the previous principle in (Strichartz, 2000) where I thought I had seen it before (see pp. 17–18), in fact, in Berlin as that was where I read most of his book shortly after I arrived there in the beginning of the fall of 2008. It's not mentioned.

At any rate, puzzled as I am, I should tell you the principle is immensely helpful. Attribution of the nature discussed here is reminiscent of Schumann believing his musical compositions were dictated to him by Beethoven (Carson, 2011). If you are a researcher, to be convinced of the merit of what I am describing try the following experiment: View a problem you are working on under the prism of a friend, preferably working on a different area; for example, commit yourself to contact them to facilitate your change in perspectives, but try to do so afterward (it's tricky).

In closing this discussion, let me discuss rationalization with respect to art. Can art be rationalized? The question sounds dubious on the surface as if I am pondering the extent to which there is an algorithm that can create music better than Beethoven. In my opinion, we are far from that state although that computers can play chess better than Kasparov is not something we should take for granted (a posteriori value judgments can differ substantially from their a priori counterparts as Oded Goldreich remarks by virtue of having received the Knuth prize this year.[4]).

To understand what is at stake a more accessible way to frame the previous question can be: Is creativity reproducible? American poet laureate W.S. Merwin thinks the answer is no, in that every time he writes a poem he is never sure he will be able to write another one. Actually this poem of his is one of my favorites:

Your absence has gone through me

Like thread through a needle.

Everything I do is stitched with its color.

But I disagree with Merwin: Creativity is reproducible in my opinion.

3.5 ORGANIZATION SHOULD BE ROBUST TO ERRORS

An important aspect of organization concerns its *error management principles*. On one hand, viewing errors as strokes of luck has the negative impact that an

---

4 See: https://rjlipton.wordpress.com/2017/06/22/oded-wins-the-knuth-prize/.

organization misses out on important opportunities for corrective action. On the other, understanding errors as flaws in the nature of the respective actors anathematizes both organizations and actors alike. What we, thus, propose is to follow a *Goldilocks principle*[5] in the design of organizations in that, in the interest of pursuing of truth in organizational matters, we should look somewhere in the middle between these extremes.

Organizational design can take place in a spectrum of approaches between two extremes: (1) The paradigm of the Biblical Commandments oriented around implicating negative behavior and, in this way, inciting ecclesiastical and state institutions to rely on severe penalties to police behavior. (2) The incipient stages of the internet infrastructure built around trusted users and operators (for example, protocols trusting the components involved in their execution to do the "right thing" [follow specifications]).

Of course these approaches differ in their properties: On one hand, what we may call the *biblical paradigm* suppresses negative behavior at the expense of inducing a sense of paranoia among organizational actors in feeling the presence of God (and by extension ecclesiastical and state institutions that are organized according to the paradigm of the commandments) from a negative perspective. This acts contrary to the development of an affinity for divinity and entices those who follow the Christian, for example, faith to displace divinity outside of their psychic purview into the heavens.

Organizing according to the biblical paradigm has the side effect of stifling innovation: Organizational actors that are obligated to follow rigid protocols as they carry out their work (and being perpetually wary that deviations are heavily penalized) naturally tend to avoid innovative (and, thus, error-prone) approaches in their respective organizational tasks.

That the industrial age placed (and, to some extent, modern societies continue to place) severe ethical penalties on errors can, in my opinion, be attributed to the fact that the population has been accustomed to the idea that *sinful acts*, commonly understood as an inexorable trait of human existence, lead to condemnation. Sins easily admit an interpretation as errors in following the Biblical Commandments and Christian morality, thus the confusion. Furthermore, I believe that what is also at stake in this confusion is the weaving of the concept of *contractual obligations*, necessary for an industrial economy to function properly, with Christian morality in that contract violations correspond to an analogue sinful acts (that deserve being severed heavy penalties).

---

5 See: https://rjlipton.wordpress.com/2017/05/30/goldilocks-principle-and-p-vs-np/.

On the other hand, the paradigm followed in the development of the internet enabled the internet infrastructure to develop fast, but the population of operating networks and end users increased, issues of safety and security came into play that were addressed in a fashion that in many ways started acting against the foundational principles of the internet architecture. For example, monitoring equipment (such as *firewalls*) policed traffic to prevent the proliferation of malware but such policing had the negative side effect that innovation started becoming ever more cumbersome.

Getting to the question of how organizations can stimulate creativity, note to that end that *tolerance for errors* seems necessary for any creative venture to succeed. Quoting Einstein: "Anyone who has never made a mistake has never tried anything new." The contrapositive of Einstein's thought is that to try something new you have to expect mistakes in your task. Looked at from this latter perspective, Einstein speaks of something evident for anyone who has tried out using paper and pencil a new idea in the interest of solving a mathematical problem. It is an unfortunate but blunt reality that as students make mistakes in their homework, they are prone to attribute these mistakes to limitations of their ability to do math rather than a phenomenon in creative ventures. Einstein's quote is not obvious for a majority of people. We should, thus, ponder how to change that.

We have insofar discussed the notion of an error extensively. Let us now draw our attention to the related concept, namely, that of a *fault*. I use the term as a deviation from an organizational protocol. That is, I deem errors as deviations from what is true in statements involving an argument of reason and faults as *protocol deviations* in organizational function. Viewing creative output from organizational actors as faulty computation, I believe that the mathematical theory of distributed computing and, in particular, the theory of *Byzantine fault tolerance* can be brought to bear in the design of organizations: Faults can be classified in a spectrum from being simple (such as a *crash* in a computing system in the sense that the system fails and stop working) to being the complex situations that manifest as organizational elements act adversarially against the system (organization) to thwart correct execution even if troubleshooting efforts have being initiated (as Byzantine elements will try to thwart them). The term Byzantine is understood in computer science as an infinitely powerful opponent, in the sense that his or her behavior can be arbitrarily adversarial (of course subject to the operational constraints of the system). The challenge is to build robustness in the organizational protocols without compromising on the creative nature of organizational output.

The implications that trying out new things entail errors and faults in their execution go beyond pure mathematics: Looking at Silicon Valley, for example, the success rate of Silicon Valley startups can be as low as 10%.[6] The culture of Silicon Valley tries to rejoice in entrepreneurial failures to the extent possible in the interest of learning lessons leading to success. As Greece is developing its entrepreneurial environment, there are important lessons to be learned in this regard.

But there are other implications that warrant careful investigation: The success rates in entrepreneurship an economy can sustain reflect on economic indicators (that summarize the economy). In Greece, fluctuations in these indicators are closely monitored by European institutions at the risk of speculative corrective action by the European Central Bank, for example, that can fall outside the purview of the Greek government. Furthermore, European pacts aggressively (and arbitrarily) dampen such fluctuations (by design).[7] It is not unlikely the Greek crisis was, in fact, triggered by speculative action acting against the creative character of our economy and what is even more troubling is that the same thing can happen again.

To foster creativity implies a significant paradigm shift in organization: Organizational output has to adjust to employee contributions, rather than the other way round (corresponding to hiring employees to develop the products senior level management has a priori decided should be developed). To a large extent, the mentality of adjusting to the work that is produced by employees exists in prestigious research labs in the United States. But these research labs are typically slashed whenever a corporation faces economic hardship and research personnel either leaves the organization to pursue careers elsewhere or becomes narrowly focused to the products an organization provides. I am, thus, tempted to ask: What would it take to stabilize research pursuits in large and small organizations? I leave this as a question for future work.

---

6 https://www.theguardian.com/technology/2014/jun/28/silicon-valley-startup-failure-culture-success-myth.

7 Alan Kirman's interview to the Crisis Observatory of ELIAMEP (Greece): http://crisisobs.gr/en/2016/06/sinentefxi-tou-alan-kirman-epitimos-kathigitis-ikonomikon-sto-aix-marseille-iii-university/.

4

THE STIGMATA OF UNACCOUNTABLE PRESENCE

I was graduate student at Princeton as a fleeting paper deadline served as an impetus for a challenging implementation problem. I do not have expert experience in implementing software in any particular environment or domain, but within a few days I found myself trying to implement a variety of protocols I had developed in my research in a platform at the cluster facility of the Computer Science Department at Princeton. One of the most challenging tasks I had to face involved debugging: As bugs for code being executed in one machine depended on versions of the software running in other machines, localizing the errors was cumbersome. The situation I soon entered can only be mildly described as chaotic. I had gone to great lengths to add redundancy in my code to facilitate debugging and I was also using software designed for that specific purpose (I had kindly asked the system administrators to install in the platform I was using for my experimentation).

But in spite of my efforts, the error was managing to miraculously escape my localization efforts: As I was trying to hone in on the lines where the errors I was looking for might have been at, my efforts were persistently being rendered futile at the 11th hour. (The nature of the error must have been of a different kind than the kind of error I was expecting to find.) But at the 12th (on the next day), my debugging effort came to a successful end after replacing my implementation of a *heap data structure* with one I found on the internet: I had made a mistake in translating the logic in the pseudocode implementation Cormen et al. (1990) have on heaps to executable code in C/C++ (the programming language I was using). The bottom line is that a simple error in logic can wreak such havoc in a distributed system that nothing but a prayer can appease the ensuing hell.

In virtue of my model in this monograph that organizations are a version of distributed computing systems, what this model strongly suggests is that the algorithms (organizational principles and day-to-day organizational practices) running our economies are more often than not buggy and that the efforts to localize and correct errors certainly seem related to my futile effort to localize a structural error to a particular line of code. Random as the behavior that manifests in a distributed system with implementation errors becomes, and drawing on the analogy with organizations as distributed systems, that we often attribute agency in the manifestation of random phenomena[1] could act as an explanation of the conspiracy theories that plague the capitalist system.

4.1 ORGANIZATION BASED ON EMULATION

Roar

–Katy Perry

A fundamental building block of organization without formal commitments is a *perspective*. As a case in point, we use the mathematical model of the *stag hunt*, an archetypical game-theoretic model of coordination (a notion closely related to organization). To that end, let us introduce elementary background in game theory that we build on to give a formal definition of the stag hunt.

4.1.1 Strategic Games and Their Analysis

Let us begin with the definition of games in (finite) *strategic form* (also called a *normal form*). To define a game in this form, we need to specify the set of players, the set of strategies available to each player, and a utility function for each player whose domain is all possible combinations of strategies that determine a player's payoff. Formally, a strategic-form game Γ is a triple

$$\Gamma = \left(I, (S_i)_{i \in I}, (u_i)_{i \in I}\right)$$

where $I = \{1, \ldots, n\}$ is the set of players, S_i is the set of pure strategies available to player i, and $u_i: S \to \mathbb{R}$ is the utility function of player i where $S = X_i S_i$ is the set of all strategy profiles (combinations of strategies). We often wish to vary

---

[1] For example, see this TED talk by Michael Shermer: https://www.youtube.com/watch?v=8T_jwq9ph8k.

the strategy of a single player while holding other players' strategies fixed. To that end, we let s_{-i} denote a strategy selection for all players but i, and write (s'_i, s_{-i}) for the profile

$$(s_1, \ldots, s_{i-1}, s'_i, s_{i+1}, \ldots, s_n)$$

A pure strategy profile σ^* is a *Nash equilibrium* if, for all players i,

$$u_i(\sigma^*_i, \sigma^*_{-i}) > u_i(s_i, \sigma^*_{-i}) \text{ for all } s_i \epsilon S_i$$

That is, a Nash equilibrium is a strategy profile such that no player can obtain a larger payoff using a different strategy while the other players' strategies remain fixed. The previous definitions concern Nash equilibria in pure strategies; however, we note that Nash equilibria admit an analogous definition assuming players may use *mixed strategies,* that is, probability distributions over their respective pure strategy sets. Nash equilibria in mixed strategies are known to always exist in strategic form games (Nash, 1950, 1951), in contrast to pure Nash equilibria.

4.1.2 The Stag Hunt

The *stag hunt* is a well-known *coordination game* capturing essential aspects of organization that we draw on in our study. Skyrms (2004) defines the stag hunt as follows: "Let us suppose that the hunters [in a group] each have just the choice of hunting hare or hunting deer. The chances of getting a hare are independent of what others do. There is no chance of bagging a deer by oneself, but the chances of a successful deer hunt go up sharply with the number of hunters. A deer is much more valuable than a hare. Then we have the kind of interaction that is now generally known as the stag hunt."

In the stag hunt, each player has two pure strategies, one cooperative and one that corresponds to defection from cooperation (playing solitaire). Playing the cooperative strategy without cooperation from others renders a payoff inferior to defection (as it induces one's energy to go down from pursuing an unsuccessful hunt). Choosing to defect earns a player a small nutritious value irrespective of what others do. The stag hunt has two Nash equilibria in pure strategies, namely, universally adopting the superior cooperative strategy and universally defecting from using that strategy. The manifestation of the latter equilibrium is known as a *coordination failure*. The stag hunt also has a mixed Nash equilibrium providing payoffs inferior to those of either of the pure Nash equilibria, deemed unstable, and generally ignored in the literature.

4.1.3 The Power of Commitments in Organization

Organization, from our perspective in this monograph, is concerned with the computational effort and processes required to reap *coordination opportunities* (for example, universal cooperation in a stag hunt). A hunt, for example, is a computational process and, from a pragmatic perspective, the outcome is not sure to produce positive results. In the model of the stag hunt, these computational issues are defined away in assuming that if all players join forces, the outcome is sure to be successful whereas if few enough players join in hunting, the outcome is known to be a coordination failure.

Being interested in the organizational aspects of the stag hunt, there is a further matter needing attention: On a successful hunt, the nutritious value must be shared among the hunters in proportion to their effort. In the game-theoretic model, this issue is also defined away by fixing the payoffs each player receives should all players choose to cooperate. To realize this assumption from the organizational perspective concerning us here, we need the notion of a *commitment*.

A commitment between a corresponding organization (which may have a legal or other character) and each individual being a member of that organization is typical. With this in mind, we may distinguish between the *precommitment* phase of organizing, whose study leads us to theorize about the formation of organizations, and the *postcommitment* phase, whose study leads to theorize about the success (and failure) of organizational missions. This monograph's main focus is on the study of postcommitment organizational operation, but the precommitment phase is important to understand an organization's lifecycle and to understand what is at stake at the incipient stages of organization.

Coming back to the stag hunt, commitments between the players on how the possible quarry will be shared would relieve doubts from the hunters the great effort they have to contribute would be rewarded and it would reinforce trust in a fashion that would benefit the hunting efforts.

4.1.4 The Power of Forcing a Perspective of Power

Let us recall that the stag hunt has two equilibria in pure strategies as plausible outcomes, namely, universal cooperation in hunting stag and universal defection in hunting hare. Which equilibrium is selected depends on a factor called *coordination risk* in the sense that each player is uncertain on which strategy other players will choose. If a player believes other players will hunt hare, he or she is better off likewise hunting hare. The situation is analogous in the decision to hunt stag. Thus, perspectives are the decisive factor in the equilibrium the hunting group selects. The stag hunt is an archetypical model of *emulation* in that the pursuit of the superior outcome is driven by the desire to succeed in challenging and worthy ventures. If each player in a stag hunt engages in forcing a perspective of power to the rest of the players, the chances of the superior equilibrium being selected by the group go up sharply as a windfall of emulation becomes reinforced. Unfortunately, forcing perspectives of power becomes harder as the size of the group increases. Thus, organization in large groups cannot rely on emulation alone – commitments gain plausibility to facilitate organization.

4.2 DELEGATION AND MISDELEGATION

Let me now explore one elementary primitive that can be used to bind individuals in the form of organizations as well as to bind organizations together in higher level organizational forms. The primitive is that of *delegation* defined as the act of assigning executive responsibility for the implementation of a task to one individual or organization on the principles, instruction, or specification of another individual or organization. Delegation can also manifest as an organizational primitive in the form of a relationship between an individual (such as an emperor) and a corresponding *divine entity*. Examples of delegation manifest in the political representation of citizens in parliament in the system of governance known as the *republic,* the assignment of a public project such as the construction of a public road to a contractor, and the assignment of a post (such as secretarial support) to an employee of the state (civil servant) or an employee of a corporate (business) organization.

Delegation is an organizational primitive deeply ingrained in human thought. To a great extent, delegation is a primitive every human being experiences starting from the moment their conscious life begins (that moment could be anywhere after inception, into gestation, up to shortly after birth) in their relationship with their parents (who assume rearing responsibility). That such parental relationships can be strong enough to shape the thinking of an individual throughout his or her life even after parental responsibility to cater for one's upbringing ceases to be dominant in their life is something Sophocles explores in his renowned Oedipus Rex and Electra.

Delegation has been studied from a mathematical perspective in economic theory in what is referred to as the *agency model* (for example, see (Laffont &

Martimort, 2002)) in a fashion that considers delegation as a sine qua non in the organization of the economy. In economic theory, delegation involves the assignment of work in exchange for a monetary compensation. However, monetary compensation is notoriously difficult to get right in laboratory experiments.[2] Nevertheless, delegation is a powerful technique to synthesize solutions to social problems. Consider, for example, the phenomenon of *the tragedy of the commons,* a well-known problem in *collective action* coined by William Forster Lloyd and also Hardin (1968). In the archetypical example where the tragedy of the commons manifests, there is a grazing land and shepherds who use this land to feed their herds. Without restrictions in feeding one's flock, every shepherd is incentivized to overfeed their respective herd leading to depletion of the nutrients. (When there are two shepherds the problem has the structure of a *two-player prisoner's dilemma.*)

In a manner similar to how a *binding contract* can solve the prisoner's dilemma (in that the superior cooperative outcome (equilibrium) is selected), a trusted party delegating the right to graze in the farmland to the shepherds can solve the tragedy of the commons. That is not to say this is the only solution to this riddle, but it demonstrates the power of delegation. As another example, delegating the resolution of a dispute to impartial judicial authorities is indisputably desirable. Problems can arise though from *misdelegation*, that is, when there is mismatch between what the person delegating a task desires and what the person being delegated that task can and does implement.

The failure of the communist model of organization of the state can be attributed to misdelegation: The distribution of individual reward from aggregate output was delegated to the state, who proved grossly incapable of fairly distributing the reward according to individual contribution, and workers did not have an incentive to live up to their contribution potential (far from it).

The notion of rational justice is quite relevant in the aforementioned communist failure but also comes out in the following dilemma: If a person delegates a task to another and the latter is successful, who deserves the most credit? The former has to be credited with the ingenuity of having selected someone fit for the role but shouldn't the latter's effort in adjusting and being productive through that role be rewarded? It is also certainly possible that the latter actor considered it an honor to be appointed to the task at hand by, say, a higher rank official, and that sense of pride reinforced his efforts. To whom is the reward to be accorded then?

---

[2] See Dan Ariely's talk at TEDxBlackRockCity on "Money changes everything."

The situation I just described involved a successful delegation decision, but, more often than not, errors plague delegation and in such situations it is often not clear where the error or fault is to be ascribed to.

For example, most athletes, even ones working in solo, have a coach. If an athlete's coach encourages that athlete to be treated with illegal doping treatment, it is certainly the athlete's responsibility to refuse but then would his or her performance disqualify him or her from winning medals in sports events, especially if doping treatment is the norm in the environment wherein the athlete competes? And if the athlete is caught in doping tests, who is to blame for the failure of living up to excellence in this profession? In hindsight, how can an athlete select a coach that will help him live up his true potential? Of course other types of errors are possible in such professional relationship. As an aside, Spyros Louis, the only Greek gold medalist (a medal earned in the Olympic marathon) in the Athens Olympic games of 1896 to my knowledge did not have a coach.

Analogous coaching situations manifest in academia. As I was a student in the United States, I had difficulties building good relationships with my advisors. What an advisor can offer to a graduate student depends on a variety of factors such as whether he has tenure, what research funds he or she has at his or her disposal, how engaged he is with his colleagues, whether he has a good understanding of the problem/topic a student is working on, etc. Perhaps most importantly, an advisor should develop a genuine interest in caring about his or her student to solve good problems and advance in their career. I recall Professor Ioannis Diamesis's advice in responding to my expressed desire to continue with graduate studies in the United States, that I should find an advisor who will care for me. I had wondered back then: How can I find an advisor that doesn't care? I didn't pay attention to Diamesis's advice as I had not understood how to go about following that advice: Aligning the incentives of an advisor and an advisee is a darn hard problem.

Let me continue with the alignment between an advisor and an advisee. The only time the issue was directly addressed in conversation was with my counselor at Princeton, Dr. Marvin Geller. I recall complaining about Jewish impact on the world at large, and after he managed to appease my distress, he told me: "I will act in your best interest." His ascertainment marks, I dare say, an epoch in my understanding of human relationships. In my opinion, what is at stake in asymmetric relationships to achieve alignment of incentives must be explicitly discussed between the parties being involved. If anyone delegates a task to me, I would want to know how he or she will benefit from the task I am about to execute – there are things that are obvious but none should be silent.

Let me now discuss an article on *outsourcing inspiration to endusers* by Adam Grant.[3] Businesses typically draw their inspiration from their employees, especially those executives at the upper echelon of the corporate hierarchy. Grant gives examples, however, that end users of final products can be a great source of inspiration, especially as customers interact directly with product developers. Business hierarchies can act contrary to this interaction, however: Grant points out that executives may try to prevent end users interacting with product developers as such interaction can act antagonistically to their corporate role (of being inspiration drivers for their businesses).

4.3 RELIGIOUS ASPECTS OF DELEGATION

Individuals observing a religious faith, as they venture in life, often ascribe to their professional mission proportions of religious order. For example, in Greek culture, where Orthodox Christianity is the dominant religion and a majority of Greeks are faithful, it is perhaps not a coincidence that failure is highly culpable evoking feelings akin to those evoked by the commitment of a sinful act. Unwitting of the collective effort required for a professional post or mission to be successful, many Greeks are pliable to assume disproportionate responsibility for a failure at the risk of their well-being or even life. Of course, this phenomenon is not peculiar to Greek culture (cf. Japanese seppuku).

This phenomenon is not unrelated to a cognitive schema I call *submission to God*, a manifestation of which is portrayed in the film *Conan the Barbarian*[4] wherein a religious leader, Thulsa Doom, demonstrates tour de force by instructing a follower to commit suicide. The death of the follower in the fashion it takes place is an exhibition of *vainglory power* before a promised crucifixion of Conan (that will fail). There are organizations where analogous exhibitions of vainglory power routinely take place as there are many crucifixions in contemporary professional environments that succeed.

4.4 DELEGATION AND HIERARCHIES

Let us now discuss hierarchical delegation in detail. An act of delegation is characterized by an asymmetric relationship between the persons involved:

---

3 See: https://hbr.org/2011/06/how-customers-can-rally-your-troops.
4 See: https://www.youtube.com/watch?v=P2EQ0FlVks4.

The person delegating is typically assumed to be of higher stature than the person being delegated (a corresponding task). This asymmetry is perhaps the single most important reason for the prevalence of hierarchies in organization: A hierarchy prevents a chain of commands by which a person of lower stature (rank in the hierarchy) delegates a task to one of higher stature. We analyze the perils of delegation as issues emanating from moral hazard (in that the individual delegating a task is inclined to take more risk because the ensuing cost is bore by the individual being delegated the task) and related ethical dilemmas.

4.4.1 The Neural System of a Hierarchical Organization

Hierarchies are an elementary concept in mathematics, in science, and computer science, in particular. At the beginning of an internship at Akamai Technologies (which I also discuss later in this book that took place in the meantime between my first and second academic years at Princeton), I recall trying to learn the basics of Akamai's main product through discussion with coworkers. The main product was a *caching service* implemented through a network of *storage devices* (that is, caches) strategically deployed in the internet's infrastructure that were uploaded with World Wide Web content (such as images) to minimize the network distance between users (downloading) and web servers (uploading). In particular, I recall a meeting where Akamai's of a *cache hierarchy* was discussed (as that was used in the design and implementation of their caching service).

As a parenthesis, I should say the concept of a cache hierarchy was familiar to me prior to that internship, and to a great extent even before my graduate studies: I vividly recall trying to convince a friend and classmate, as I was working on my *diploma thesis* at NTUA on *mobile agents* and *code mobility*, that it would certainly be beneficial to build an infrastructure that dynamically replicates content (I mentioned *images* actually) for the benefit of moving that content closer to the users. I hadn't thought about the data structure of a hierarchy as an implementation option.

Coming back, what had struck me as interesting in that meeting is that, as I was inquiring on the details of how Akamai's cache hierarchy worked back then, a coworker asked me to visualize the storage devices serving as caches at the upper levels of the hierarchy as "bigger and more powerful" than those devices in the lower levels. In responding that this doesn't make sense to me, he acknowledged that indeed all caches were (roughly) build out of the same processors.

Organizations are typically structured according to a tree whose vertices correspond to organizational members and whose arcs correspond to the directions where delegation commands are issued. This tree can be understood as a *neural system* for the respective organizations, and for the majority of cases it resembles a *command and control system* akin to that used in military operations. Forcing perspectives of power is crucial to the functioning of a hierarchical organization as actors high in rank are assumed as more powerful than those in the lower ranks. Hierarchies are typically coupled with the moral code that a subordinate should not assign a task to a superior imposing severe restrictions on the nature and efficiency of the tasks that can be implemented in this fashion. We elaborate on these issues as the discussion proceeds, but let us focus first on positive aspects.

4.4.2 Looking for Merits and Workarounds in Hierarchical Organization

Hierarchical organization will not vanish any time soon in spite of the limitations. So let me try to look first into how hierarchies can benefit organization. As discussed earlier, hierarchies can benefit individuals who try to learn a profession and there are typically (in advanced industrialized societies) mechanisms in place that reward those that learn well in that there is an effort to help them climb up the hierarchy. For example, there are many stories in American corporate history of individuals who started low in that hierarchy and managed through *achievement* to reach the highest corporate ranks. I consider this to be a case of organizational hierarchies trying to reach the "smartness capacities" of its smartest members. (But there is also an important limitation of hierarchical organization: The contribution potential of the organization's members is only limited to the tasks they have been appointed to execute.) Gaining visibility as an employee through outstanding achievement does not work in Greek society. For example, Lefteris Tzanoudakis used to often recount in class that in the social hierarchies *it is corks that float*.

With respect to the army, which is based to the extent of my knowledge on strict hierarchical organization around the world (albeit with some exceptions as my understanding is that in Middle East operations hierarchical organization is somewhat lessened in the US Army), I recently heard on a Greek television program the Commander in Chief of the Greek army address the Greek people with a change in policy that military planning will no longer be based on organization around threats but will rather emphasize thinking on military issues as the main part of its planning and organization process. I find this is an important shift in focus that can leverage the thinking potential of commanders and military personnel in the possible defiance of hierarchical delegation.

The theory that hierarchical delegation can harm an ego explains a phenomenon I had found it difficult to adjust to on continuing my educational pursuits in the United States (from Greece). The phenomenon was an inherent inclination, as I had observed it, of American speakers to exhibit implicit methods of engaging in conversation (vis-á-vis the more direct approach of the Greeks). I became more comfortable with this phenomenon after ascribing to the American mentality the positive intent (in implicit conversational engagement) of permitting greater "slack" to the thinking and ensuing actions of the partner in conversation, an explanation which worked for me in practical matters in my life as a graduate student quite well. The previous theory quite strongly affirms this prior explanation: Although organization in the United States is inexorably hierarchical (lacking any better organization methods), the American people are decentralized and such implicit (but, typically, logically clear) methods of engagement simply enrich social discourse and output.

4.4.3 Limitations and Stigmata of Hierarchies: Limited Number of Good Positions

It is a plain fact that there is inequality all around the world even in industrialized nations. But viewing the economy as a collection of corporations each with its own hierarchical system of organization, the inequality that is observed around the world is no surprise: There are only a limited number of positions in the economy that can afford an affluent lifestyle in comparison to the entire population. At the same time, the economic system in the fashion it is organized delegates responsibility to each individual to climb up the hierarchy. The individuals that try to do so face a sclerotic organizational structure that resists their efforts. The structural barriers for citizens in the lower echelon of society to climb up the hierarchical ladders is discussed in public dialogue by former President Barack Obama, who points out the need to ameliorate the resistance. Let me point out that the issue we are facing (as thinkers and academics) is not about capital (or capitalism) per se but rather with the fashion that capital is allocated to the organizational actors in society.

In my opinion, capitalism is a great system for the organization of wealth production granted there is leeway for the flow of capital between economic actors – in my opinion, it is the sclerosis of hierarchies that prevents the correct functioning of capitalism. After the fall of the Soviet bloc, the idea that capitalism would prevail as a global system for the organization of economic activity nourished my dreams of undertaking entrepreneurial activity in areas of the Soviet bloc where Greeks had a long time presence throughout their history. I was not rich in capital, but I was making plans I would gradually buy the company I would be employed by out of salary savings. When much later the possibility of being given stock options at Akamai Technologies was put on the table, a version of these earlier dreams became ever more resonant. I should say I could have easily seen my life as having been branched in a fashion similar to how Warren Buffett's did.

4.4.4 The Battleground for Limited Resources

Rather than nourishing dreams of commerce and value exchange, our economic system drives economic output by creating situations where we must compete to ensure *access to resources* be those jobs, food, or mating. Viewing the economy as a resource allocation apparatus is problematic and hierarchies do nothing but perpetuate that perspective. The study of racism in these terms is worthwhile: Thinking racism as a system of social classification whose goal is to provide access to the limited number of jobs (and related resources) in a hierarchically organized economy to a dominant race while excluding those who belong to other races from competing for favorable conditions of access to the limited resources is a worthwhile pursuit. Certainly, as the economy tightens its noose racism thrives (for example, in Greece), whereas in economic boons it appears to be nearly absent.

4.4.5 Limitations and Stigmata of Hierarchies: Delegation Chains and Debugging

A vexing issue in hierarchical organization is a separation between executive decisions and the work that is required for these decisions to be implemented (a process that can progress along possibly long *delegation chains* across multiple hops in a hierarchy). The issue is important even from a legal perspective as the responsibility for the execution of a task is distributed along a possibly large number of actors and it is not clear how to ascribe liability for wrongdoings. The issue is addressed differently in French and German bureaucracies for public administration where in the former case the liability lies with the manager who is delegating a task whereas in the latter the liability lies with the inferior in rank employee being delegated a task. However, the difficulty of localizing errors in the decision and implementation process applies to either administration system.

4.4.6 The Architectural Stigma of Having a Single Point of Failure

As a graduate student at Princeton into the beginning of my PhD program, I was interested in studying computer system performance, a subject many computer scientists had been working on. But that changed in my second year as I was taking a course by Professor Randy Wang, who astutely observed in class that no matter how good the performance of a system is, if the system stops working, you get a performance of zero. This was an idea I wanted to explore, and, in doing so, I recall evaluating the distributed computing systems we were studying in class from the perspective of failures. In this process, I realized that most systems were vulnerable whether to random faults but especially security attacks. I realized that robustness was a wonderful topic for exploration.

Thus, last but not least, we come to the most important limitation of hierarchical organization, namely, that systems designed hierarchically typically have a *single point of failure* at the root of the corresponding tree that conceptually describes the system's organization. A single point of failure can lead to catastrophic collapse that no computer system designer would ever want to confront (whether under analytic scrutiny or in operation under the test of time). Nevertheless, as mentioned earlier, the majority, if not all, organizations operate under hierarchical principles of management.

4.5 ERRORS IN ORGANIZATION

Hierarchical organization cannot rest on placing an infallible individual at the root of the hierarchical tree since, as we argue in the rest of this section, human nature is possibly inexorably fallible.

4.5.1 Can a Flawed Nature Exist?

There is indisputably an innate proclivity in our nature to make errors. This proclivity urges many of us to attribute these errors to flaws in our nature in the sense that we, as human beings, are lesser than an infallible divine nature that, for example, Christianity assumes to form an essential part of the essence of God. That God is infallible and that humans should perpetually aspire to elevate the state of their existence in congruity with the ideal of God's divinity are essential elements of Christian morality that seem to imply, by common sense, that it is reasonable for human beings to strive to be infallible. For example, struggling in homework, at all levels of education, often makes students envious of a state of their intellectual nature whereby homework is easy.

But there are alternative explanations of human errors as there are theories of the cosmos. As for the latter, that infallibility is an essential element of divinity is hardly true in the religious traditions of the Greeks prior to Christianity. As a case in point, Themis, the Titaness whose name the Greek word for institution derives from, was established as the goddess of divine justice by virtue of her foresight. In contrast, in the philosophical tradition of the (modern) West, one that has been soundly influenced by Catholicism, a branch of Christianity that departs in many respects from the Greek tradition of Orthodoxy,[5] a matter of long enduring debate is if and to what extent the assumption of *free will*, as a property of human nature, is in accordance with God's infallibility, by virtue of *divine providence*, but also if it makes sense at all to assume God has free will himself.[6] In my opinion, it is highly unclear to what extent, if at all, Christ attributes infallibility to God.

Let us come now to the issue of alternative explanations of human errors other than an inherently flawed nature. To that end, we challenge ourselves with the following question: Consider a being whose nature is *perfect*. Can that being make *errors* and what might be their purpose? Our thought experiment is ill-defined, so let us make a few additional *assumptions* (or *frames of truth* as Richard Feynman has referred to them in public debate in his eloquent and accessible style of debate[7]). Our first assumption amounts to a rather narrow definition of error as a *mathematical error*. So, for example, an error of this nature can be one in *algebra*. Or, alternatively, an error can be one in *programming a Turing machine*. Our second assumption is about the definition of a perfect nature.

In my opinion, humans are unlikely to be bounded in computation by the model of a Turing machine, but a variety of academics, in fact, the vast majority of them, think otherwise: A commonly held belief among computer scientists is that the aforementioned Church-Turing thesis is true. In this way,

---

[5] See this talk by r. Nikolaos Loudovikos: https://www.youtube.com/watch?v=yuQOa2h87oM.
[6] See: https://plato.stanford.edu/entries/divine-freedom/.
[7] See: https://www.youtube.com/watch?v=36GT2zI8lVA&t=20s.

they more or less attribute to the Turing machine the status of representing the perfect nature of cognitive capacity on par with the religious (and philosophical) tenet that the perfect nature of God is what humans should strive to attain. I do not claim computer scientists think of Turing machines as infallible (the statement doesn't make sense), nevertheless, the fear that *artificial intelligence* will supplant human cognition is not only permeant among computer scientists but the presumably superior nature of the Turing machines vis-á-vis our cognitive skills has even permeated the judiciary (in how machine learning factors in judicial decisions).

On these grounds it is reasonable, for the purposes of the argument I hereby try to construct, to assume perfect nature that of a Turing machine. But then immediately the infallibility of a perfect nature becomes nothing more than an oxymoron by the HALTING theorem. More precisely, even if a perfect nature exists, it is impossible to prove so. In other words, what my simple argument has managed to reveal is that the Church-Turing thesis and the assumption of Christianity (and Western philosophy) that an infallible divine nature exists cannot be simultaneously true. Stated bluntly, there is a lot of debate, especially in the circles of the church,[8] on whether humans evolved (cf. intelligent design versus Darwinian evolution). All of a sudden, the philosophical debate on human evolution is not so important as if I construct in my garage a device that falsifies the Church-Turing thesis, it is highly unclear what the fate of humanity is going to be.

Furthermore, whether an infallible nature exists and whether humans can ever reach such a state of existence is also highly unclear. I am not sure I can even frame the question correctly but posing it in the following fashion makes sense: I continue to assume mathematics as the frame whereby errors are defined. I also assume that errors are programming errors. But in which mathematical model of computing machine? Let us assume for the sake of our thought experiment that there exists a computational model that is more powerful than a Turing machine in that it can compute anything a Turing machine can compute with comparable efficiency but it can compute more in that there exist algorithmic problems that can be solved in this model that do not admit efficient solutions in Turing machines. For example, say that in such a model the HALTING problem as that is defined for Turing machines admits an efficient solution. Considering a generic computational model with this property, it is natural to ask if there is anything the model cannot compute.

---

8 For the perspective of Richard Dawkins, see https://www.youtube.com/watch?v=6u8gAV7om_g.

This question lies at the heart of the HALTING theorem and it is a testament of Turing's genius.

Searching for this Holy Grail of computation is interesting, but in my opinion this pursuit has little to do with whether human nature is flawed or not. The fact that human nature can pose these questions is a testament of its faculty. But my monograph is one on organization rather than the exploration of a true meaning of infallibility. Feynman was often hostile to meaningless philosophy.[9] I do not agree hostility against philosophy is a prolific line of discourse, but I am also interested, as Feynman is, in progress. To that end, in placing errors in the realm of organizational design, I draw on my experience with mathematical problem-solving as I draw on that of others.

4.5.2 Success, Failure, Rejection, and Guilt

Success is so important for us in the West it is interesting to ask to what extent it could be any less important in other cultures. Before exploring this question, let me clarify that although Greece is often acknowledged as the cradle of Western civilization it is unclear to what extent Greece can be classified as being Western, Eastern, or something independent of the two. The latter possibility is what makes most sense to me. That Greece is *a world alone* would probably resonate with most Greeks as most of us would probably resonate with Lorde's perspective of what that means.[10]

As I was recently having lunch with a coworker, namely, Yuichi Yoshida, at the National Institute of Informatics in Tokyo, Japan, in asking me what the most important element of Greek culture is, I instantaneously responded that, in my opinion, it is what our flag is understood to represent: *Freedom or death*. He somewhat hesitantly responded, as I asked him back what the most important element of Japanese culture is, that the pursuit of *harmony* is what is openly hailed in Japan, an assertion that is arguably discordant with the present status of this country. Our discussion continued along the lines of observations I had made in the short period I had stayed there that in the coffee shops I used to work I had observed many fellow Japanese had, what I had understood as, symptoms of *obsessive compulsive disorder*, an anxiety disorder that typically manifests in people with high intelligence. That made me wonder as of why these people are not taking action to appease their

---

9 See an excerpt from Richard Feynman's lecture entitled "On hungry philosophers (or do we see objects or only their light)": https://www.youtube.com/watch?v=X8aWBcPVPMo.
10 See: https://www.youtube.com/watch?v=eWUnVyO1Klk.

anxiety. In my opinion, this should be an important desideratum of Japanese society.

From kindergarten to graduation from the lyceum (high school), I studied at a private school, namely, Doukas School, with the exception of the second year of Lyceum that I had spent in the public school of Melissia, the Athenian suburb I am writing these lines from.

My father was trying hard to convince me in the meantime between the second and the third year of lyceum to reregister to my former school worried as he was about my prospects in the highly competitive exams that determine which students are granted the privilege of public tertiary education. As I gave in sharing his concerns I questioned the feasibility of reregistering, but I was surprised to find out he had already taken care of that. He had been struggling with our finances in affording me the privilege to have a good private education. But his efforts panned out: Least of all, he must have felt proud my name appeared in the newspapers by virtue of my grades in the aforementioned exams. In fact, this is the only (insofar) appearance of my name in a newspaper, and important as public discussion of one's work is for American academia, I hope this will change soon. Coming back, I had felt so content in hearing the news on my performance, I told my father, as we were standing on the balcony of our apartment house, that I was so happy I wouldn't mind even if I were to die. He only smiled in response as an expression of contentment appeared alike on his face.

As a student in Doukas school, my life was mostly solitary, as was that of one of my classmates in senior year. I recall him being in the school over a period of years but our paths hadn't met until then. We were not friends but I respected his intellect. I recall punching him in class. This was technically possible without creating fuss as his desk was right in front of mine. It was not out of disrespect, we had an insignificant quarrel and that was how I felt like reacting. Neither of us bore a grudge to my knowledge. His father congratulated me after my graduation speech. The school honored me in that capacity by virtue of my grade point average in the aforementioned qualifying exams. Doukas was enormously successful that year.

He continued his education at Imperial College under a prestigious fellowship. But a few years after graduation I heard he died in a car accident in London. One mutual friend questioned the extent to which that event was random and another recounted that, in running into him in London shortly before the accident, Serapheim was unhappy and his glance empty as if he was staring into a void. It is not unlikely that mounting pressure that can be traced to before his departure to England, and in combination with those inexorable systemic bugs I have been discussing in this book, triggered grief that, in turn, triggered his misfortune. Fellow classmate, rest in peace.

Rejection, in any of its facets, indisputably signifies for a majority of people an event so important it can even be life changing. Being rejected at trying to publish your paper at, say, a prestigious conference evokes emotions (almost) every academic associates with. Similarly, being rejected by a sensational presence across from you you momentarily thought could even change your life or, alternatively, a coworker that drives you to go to work every morning, are situations that resonate emotions (almost) every human being associates with. But above and beyond rejection in the simple sense of a failed attempt, what I have come to realize is that it is not only rejection in itself that is important but it is also resistance to rejection (and its sibling, failure) betokened as an *ethical principle* that can largely determine entire life trajectories. Let me give some examples.

I had been taken aback as my PhD thesis advisor at Princeton, Professor Hisashi Kobayashi, passed on to me what I had understood, arguably correctly, as a guiding principle in his life in telling me he had never been rejected in his life except once when he proposed for the first time to his wife. The fear of rejection as an important factor shaping, e.g., professional thought emerged again in our interactions as he was advising me how to handle a matter related to an offer (or its possibility before it had materialized, I can't recall) for a summer internship – in knowing the head of the group making the offer, he attributed such fear to the head of the group making (or about to make) the offer as a plausible explanation for a matter we were discussing. I should credit Professor Kobayashi for imparting to me an understanding of the importance of rejection and related fears in guiding behavior and professional judgment. It has explained lots of things since then.

In another example, during my recent collaboration with Professor Nikos Maratos at the National Technical University of Athens (NTUA), a collaboration that helped me materialize important and long pending results in mathematical research, he informed me in a phone call that he had just received a rejection notification from the journal he had submitted his work with his student *for the first time in his career*. Professor Maratos is a senior faculty member at NTUA.

Failure, as a close sibling of rejection, was a main topic of discussion at the inaugural conference (2013) of the MIT Enterprise Forum of Greece, an organization affiliated with MIT whose mission is to facilitate the growth of the emerging (and, arguably, quite successful) startup environment in Greece. The lack of resilience of modern Greek culture to failure was, to my rejoice, addressed quite thoroughly by panelists and especially Paul English, cofounder and CTO of Kayak.com and a lecturer at MIT's Sloan School of Management, who mentioned that in the Silicon Valley's premier start-up environment entrepreneurs often fail twice or thrice before meeting success.

Rejection and failure, in the sense I have used them above, are *errors in judgment*. Silicon Valley's positive light on failure is a good starting point to discuss related matters such as that of *courtship*. The intimate relationship between issues of courtship and professional matters of organization should be clear by now and I will thus not be entirely off topic.

Upon my arrival to Greece after a tumultuous resignation from my job at Deutsche Telekom Laboratories (T-Labs) in Berlin, Germany, my friend, Charalampos Kourtzis, shared a folder of material he had collected on courtship issues, including the epiphanic scripture of Strauss (2005). Strauss abstracts important aspects of mating strategies in a coherent structure, which is illustrated with a narrative of his own personal experiences. He gives excellent advice on how to tackle mating issues throughout, advice that is often easy to follow, judging, in fact, from my own personal experience (in briefly trying them). Although I didn't develop much friction with the methods he lays out, there is one principle I distilled from the book that is quite important and quite relevant to our discussion, namely, *mating is an issue of strategy*. In particular, this means that excuses of the sort "she is way out of my league" inner voices typically echo on first rejection are quite manageable to overcome under a principled approach to mating. In this book's vocabulary, what is ultimately necessary to be successful in mating is to illuminate conscience with the light of reason.

Let me remark I often openly discuss my strategic perspective on relationships and the reaction (to my openly stating strategic thinking as my approach) is not always as positive as I would like. The reason is important. I recall a negative reaction from male friends (of British nationality who were employed, if I recall correctly, in the public sector in Britain) during a summer vacation in the island of Skyros and also a negative reaction from a female acquaintance in Athens (of Greek nationality working as a creative designer). In both cases, I discerned reactions of fear in being subjected to an umbrella of strategy in a friendship or a romantic courtship. As I understood the perspective on the other sides of the argument, the issue is fear of *leading behavior*. That a sharp intellect can evoke positive emotions appears to be a discordant perspective for many of us it seems. In my opinion, the issue at stake can in principle also apply to professional environments.

In closing the parenthesis, patterns of thought similar in nature to the cursory echo of conscience *the shy tormented youth*[11] frequently confront manifest in aspects of life other than mating and courtship, in particular, they often manifest as shy youth venture in educational and professional affairs. While I was still in Berlin, having stayed at my office throughout the night working on a paper, as the morning cracked and cleaning personnel came in, a female cleaner standing at the back of my shoulder took fright as I turned around and away from my laptop to see if I could make her task easier. Worried as I became of what might have been on display at my computer screen, I was relieved, but also at the same time astounded, to find there nothing more than mathematical text (and possibly a figure illustrating an idea).

I had come across the concept of mathematical phobia before in the past, but I had never imagined the symptoms could be that striking.

What could possibly be the causes of such mathematical phobia? I have pondered this question ever since and my thinking has concluded to something I would like to pose as a hypothesis: Outmost mathematical phobia is the product of uttermost irrationality in working and living conditions. My reasoning is that irrationality submerges the intellect to a state of existence wherein mathematical beauty poses as a threat to existence. Beauty posing as a threat to existence is something every human being (at all income levels) faces in times of financial hardship where the default behavior is to resort to savings (beauty typically being costly). As it is not hard to imagine a spillover of the guilt associated with expenses in times of financial uncertainty to things that are beautiful as a generic property irrespective of cost, it does not take a mental leap to understand my scientific hypothesis awaiting, I hope, verification or refutation by behavioral scientists.

Let us now come back to the question of the relationship between what I referred to before as the shy tormented youth with educational subjects such as mathematics (our main topic, in relation to errors). As a student is versed in the curriculum of secondary and tertiary education, he or she is faced with a complex decision problem in considering further educational curricula and career options that is highly prone to errors in judgment. For example, the impact the teaching quality (good or bad) of even a single instructor on the career path of any given student is disproportionate to the responsibility the system of education ascribes to instruction. Considering mathematics in particular, the intellectual acuity required for mathematical proficiency at all curricular levels, but especially those in secondary education we are mostly

---

11 For Amy Macdonald's perspective, see: https://www.youtube.com/watch?v=iRYvuS9OxdA.

discussing here, can easily evoke repellants of the same nature of the repellants that drive the abortion of courtship rituals, that is, on the grounds of arguments echoing as *that is way out of my league,* for example. Retractive behavior of this sort in decision-making is often attributed to British students as they eliminate themselves from studying at Cambridge or Oxford, in spite of the efforts of the faculty at these universities, as expressed, for example, by Professor Jon Crowcroft in public venues of discussion, to attract students from more diverse social backgrounds. As I was applying for graduate studies to universities in the United States, in scanning their web sites, there was content that was to a large degree intimidating as if these prestigious schools wanted to deter applicants from applying. Furthermore, discussions of the homologous phenomenon of feeling you have been accepted to prestigious graduate programs on the grounds of errors in judgment by these schools' committees, one that admittedly did not resonate strongly in me, haven't been publicly documented – I have found records of this discussion in application materials for junior faculty positions, to the credit of these academics.

Feelings of worthlessness and failure have a deeply moral basis that can trigger errors in judgment. *Guilt* is a phenomenon of moral character associated with wrongdoing. To a great extent, guilt can be understood as a projection of an action violating a moral code (important to the respective actor) to the psyche of that actor. But also thoughts can evoke feelings of that nature. Sinful behavior can certainly evoke feelings of guilt and as Esther Perel points out in a publicly available lecture[12] to be unfaithful to your spouse is a sin even as one ponders the possibility of being unfaithful. Moral codes of this nature conflict elementary human rights such as that of the *freedom of thought.* Unless I can think about the possible outcomes of an action I am about to take, how can I introspect the possible consequences in the interest of reaching good decisions?

Let me further discuss phenomena unfounded feelings of guilt trigger to the individuals experiencing them: Elizabeth Smart in describing her story of being kidnapped and then raped on a regular basis over a period of 9 months before the police found her[13] describes her feelings in the words of being broken, beyond help and hope, useless, disgusting, and that she wasn't worth saving. In fact, she said she felt envious of the children that die in kidnapping. Although Smart did not actually fail in something, these are feelings that failure in academic and professional roles can trigger in an individual. If you

---

12 https://www.youtube.com/watch?v=P2AUat93a8Q&t=21s.
13 TED talk of Elizabeth Smart: https://www.youtube.com/watch?v=h0C2LPXaEW4.

don't believe me, ask any graduate student who has had serious problems with their advisor for their perspective. These phenomena are not to be dismissed:

In the aftermath of Smart's kidnapping, Smart's mother encouraged her to prevent anger from consuming her any further and that the best punishment for those that tortured her would be a stance characterized by defiance of her foregoing torment as if that had never happened. In my opinion, this approach is fundamentally wrong. What happened to Smart is not a bad stroke of fate. Quite the contrary, misfortunes of that modality happen all the time around us, in various forms and guises, in fact, I may be the next victim for still another time as they can also rehash in Smart's life in insidious ways she cannot expect. Anyone can be a victim, prime ministers, presidents, or even countries (such as Greece). We should definitely study the patterns that manifest under pressure and torture but we should also hold those that inflict them accountable to justice.

Toward the end of my third semester at Princeton, a sequence of events some of which are traceable to my first year (as a graduate student) and others to a summer internship (in Boston) in the meantime between my first and second years, but, foremost, a failing academic relationship with my (then) new advisor, led to a psychological breakdown (characterized by a strong sense of fear and paranoia) and a *leave of absence* (that lasted one year), which I spent in Athens.

That period was certainly one of great solitude. I often felt I could not live up to the bursts of desire I had in proactively seeking a sociable life. Such feeling of considering sociability futile is something I have occasionally noticed in other people and I have often wondered what it would take to stimulate organizing principled action as a means of defusing that futility for the benefit of meaningful socialization. But what is also important about that period is that, for the first time in my life, I strongly felt how negative the impact of stereotypical thinking can be on one's life experiences as I, along with my environment, came to question the extent to which I am *sane*.

I strongly felt there was something wrong with me, an assumption that was bluntly questioned for the first at an unsuspecting time: As I was having lunch with my parents at a restaurant in Penteli in the beautiful area near the monastery, a friend of my father approached the table to greet my parents. I cannot recall whether they had already discussed my leave of absence prior to that meeting or whether that was something raised for the first time at that table, but what I vividly recall is something that threw me off in deep thought thereafter, a remark that that person addressed directly toward me: *You should look for your interest(s)*. For the first time since my episodic departure from Princeton someone was granting me the right to think strategically.

I fell in deep thought for a variety of reasons: To some extent what he had remarked is a stereotypical way of thinking in Greek society that has often been misconstrued by a variety of people, including me, as something negative. For example, I recall wondering to myself: Why shouldn't I care about others in my pursuit to understand what went wrong? The pursuit of one's interests in Greek society has often and again been blamed as the root of patterns of unethical behavior that have been held liable, for example, for the bad state of the public sector in Greece. To my knowledge, such a bad state has perpetuated since the recent (re)institution of Greece as a national state (by virtue of the successful liberation war against the Ottomans).

4.5.3 On the Perceived Futility of Mounting Against the Establishment

The morality of *opting for one's best interest*, prevalent as it is in contemporary Greek society, is, in fact, the principle forming the scientific basis of *homo economicus*. In the name of this principle, the attack against Greek bonds in 2010 that set off the implementation of the supervised austerity program, far from being accountable to an authority on the grounds of being unethical, is something Greece should have assumed responsibility for to repel (according to the established rules of financial engagement that also equate acts of providing help to the aid of impoverished people as ones of philanthropic altruism), and the fact that she couldn't is to be understood as a sign of inherent (economic) weakness. In the name of the same principle, there are narratives recounting the relevance of game theory to economic science that erroneously interpret game theory as a *theory of selfishness.*

In informal and conversational mode of thinking, selfishness is a character trait associated with *greed* in the sense of being *myopic* in one's thinking. In *strategic games,* that is, the abstract mathematical object game theory studies, it is hard to understand if and to what extent being greedy makes any sense as a lens to render practical relevance for the theory. Maybe it makes some sense in certain toy examples of games (such as the renowned *prisoner's dilemma*) but extrapolating meaning one can extract from a few particular examples to baptize an entire theory in the perspective of that particular meaning is as deleterious as the thinking associated with stereotypes can be.

The issue I am raising can be illuminated from the perspective of the theory of algorithms: Greedy algorithms are those that choose according to narrow (local) views of what is best (Sandholm, 2010; Williamson & Shmoys, 2010). Nash equilibria are combinations of strategies such that unilateral deviations from those strategies are not harmful. Although pondering unilateral deviation from an established equilibrium amounts to a local view of the strategic environment, that game theory should be reduced to the locality of this search process should clearly be attributed to the lack of understanding of what is at stake to compute an equilibrium, an aspect economic theory has entirely missed out on: Computing Nash equilibria goes beyond narrow views of local optimization.

In my opinion, *opting for one's best interest* is a great principle of social organization for as long as the principle is understood correctly: Interpreting this principle as the *greedy pursuit of one's interest* is nothing but a harmful stereotype hardly on par with game theory's foundational principle. The issue at stake is one concerning the concept of *perspective:* One should opt for their best interest but in which game?

During the aforementioned leave of absence, I spent a substantial amount of time trying to *debug* me. Although I did not necessarily see what I was doing back then as such, the perspective is not far from what I was doing: I had just experienced a dysfunctional period of psychological nature, and I was trying to figure out what was wrong. In this vein, I took up reading Steven Covey's *The seven habits of highly effective people* (in Greek) and among the things that drew my intention was his suggestion to distinguish between things within our sphere of feasibility and others that are not, in the interest of focusing on the former. I recall him mentioning climate impact as an example: What can one do to diminish our polluting impact on the environment? The answer is clearly not much, and although one should care to adopt polluting-friendly behavior, one should also try to mitigate the negative impact images of environmental damage have on their psychology (for the benefit of avoiding psychological hindrances, one cannot do much about anyway, to personal productivity). I felt good the pessimistic perspective of the world that was frequently being portrayed in media had not been having negative impact on me. It was not because I was apathetic; on the contrary, I had often been described as sensitive by others (to my bewilderment). What was it then?

Of the things that touch me deeply, the pattern manifesting as *sincere effort* gets crushed against walls of *vainglory* is arguably very important for our story. I like to picture the type of effort I am referring to as the rising of a *naval wave,* and the walls it gets crashed against as those of a *coastal fortress,* as the incandescent melody of Goldfrapp's Jo[14] echoes in the wind amid the storm raging in our victim's psyche by virtue of the mortal indolence vainglory triggers off.

---

14 See: https://www.youtube.com/watch?v=Z_BpEL1IDr4.

The pious character of my portrayal is not coincidental. Out of sheer respect for others, that rage indolence stirs up in the psyche of actors looking for an audience (to judge their work), proud as they are of their creative ideas and pursuits, confined as it must stay to prevent harm from being randomly inflicted on others, unclear as it often is as to whom the rage must be addressed to, can mount against the very motivation driving creativity and the desire for contribution. In my opinion, the most damaging stereotype, so dominantly reinforced by modern society it has found a way to infiltrate our collective subconscious, is that effort of the type I am discussing here, must necessarily be moderated by social norms characterized by *incrementalism*, in varying amounts from small to no deviations from status quo, to facilitate acceptance (of the work and the creators themselves).

Looking at my perspective from that of a human propensity for *compliance* could perhaps clarify some aspects of the phenomenon I am trying to describe. That is indeed a boring perspective, in fact, so boring my previous argument makes all the more sense. Defiance is a virtue in art, science, and mathematics and incrementalism is explicitly condemnable in academic discourse.

Coming then back to the pious nature of creativity, pious in the sense of the respect it instils in those enamored with creative pursuits (in spite of the resistance they face), the talk of Megan Phelps-Roper amply elucidates an important point I want to make. Phelps-Roper, as she describes her effort to disentangle from a morality promoting hate but clothed in the garb of Christianity,[15] captures the resistance she faced against adopting an inclusive perspective on life, inclusive in that it embraces others for who they are, by what her mother had advised her as Phelps-Roper was a small person in trying to influence her perspective against that of God: "You're just a human being my dear sweet child." Of course, the concept of God being portrayed by the religious denomination Phelps-Roper had to partake in clearly used divinity as stratagem for religious submission. That is not to say, however, that that God is any different from the God typically invoked in the religious codes of morality that have shaped and still continue to shape Western culture.

We have insofar explored how errors factor in decision-making, how the definition of errors biases decisions, and how errors can be projected to the psyche of the decision-maker.

---

15 https://www.youtube.com/watch?v=bVV2Zk88beY.

4.5.4 Deception and Errors

Let us now explore a relationship between errors and *deception*. To that end, we discuss the problem of the deliberate introduction of errors in organizational contribution and in morality codes, and discuss how such errors can escalate to dysfunctional organization. In this vein, it is both fortunate and unfortunate that a significant part of economic theory is concerned with containing deception in organizational contributions. Since most organizations are hierarchically structured relying on delegation for the execution of organizational tasks, an important part of economic theory is the aforementioned *principal-agent model* (Laffont & Martimort, 2002) and its variants that are concerned with how a principal can cope with issues of *moral hazard, adverse selection,* and other related ethical dilemmas as he or she delegates work to an agent in a contractual relationship. But I believe this mathematical work (of great aesthetic value) can be applied to the organizational models discussed in this monograph.

4.5.5 On Being an Error

Deception also manifests in a dual facet as the deliberate introduction of errors in morality codes by those in power in order to further their goals at the expense of considerable harm on civilization.

For example, Hitler reduced Jews to an error in the human race bent on eliminating them. The escalating consequences are still unresolved as the Second World War has hardly ended: Although the war ended for Germany, in the aftermath of the Holocaust, its victims, persecuted as they were from their European homeland, set out on a quest to secure their right to a homeland. The mediating force of the war's victors did not specifically account for the fate of the Jewish populations in Germany within their European homeland, as the thunderbolt the world had been hit by did not leave enough space to think through compensatory measures. Other factors could well apply: For example, it is unclear to what extent it would have been feasible to establish a Jewish nation in Europe. Furthermore, that the Jews would have been eager to try to make ends meet in an area that so brutally punished them on the grounds of their ethnicity is questionable. Instead, Jews tried hard to reconnect with their patrimonial land in Israel facing a far from trouble-free situation.

The efforts to establish the state of Israel were accompanied by much turmoil that echoes even today. The position of American foreign policy has throughout been to support the safe establishment of Israel as a sovereign state. The support has been expressed morally and demonstrated pragmatically, for example, through financial aid. For example, I recall accounts at Princeton that echo to this date of faculty members who took academic leaves of absence to fight in Israel. This support has often come at the expense of the credibility of the American nation as a global leader and a stabilizing factor in world politics. The 9/11 incident is probably not unrelated to our topic.

I was happy to hear in the words of President Donald Trump as he was recently hosted by Israeli Prime Minister Benjamin Netanyahu that the American foreign policy in the area remains in line with the maxim *never again*. But let me point out that America's foreign policy on this matter is far from blind support for Israeli interests in the Middle East or elsewhere (as many tend to misconstrue). Let me recount to that end that my friend (from Princeton) Carmella Lutmar, in expressing discomfort on how difficult it is for Israeli citizens to obtain visas for travel to the United States, was surprised to hear such tourist visas are anymore a thing of the past for Greek citizens.

The preceding discussion raises an important question: What does it take to end the Second World War? I certainly hope that the answer won't be a Third World War. I believe that to avert that we must look into mathematics (and computer science) for the benefit of building better organizations.

Let me now get to a point lying at the heart of the organization of the church:

4.5.6 Arrow's Impossibility Theorem and Infallibility

A main subject in this section is *justice,* a concept that to most Christians has a divine character as a matter of necessity for reasons that are inherent to our nature[16] as well as inherent to the error-prone organization of the judiciary (as discussed earlier). In this vein, the concept of Judgment Day is important for most Christians. I, thus, take the opportunity to address the respectable Pope Francis, in virtue of his intellect and his role in Christianity, in reference to the concept of *papal infallibility*, with respect to its possible implications on political governance. Thus, in arguing that infallibility poses concerns, I do not mean to only imply it is because *we are only human.*

I do not question that a notion of Judgment Day will be enacted. In fact, I believe it should (but I also believe that the responsibility rests within our capacity). What I would like to question though is Christianity's portrayal of a

---

16 For example, for a wonderful abstraction of how injustice can prevail over reason by Alex M.O.R.P.H. and Sylvia Tosun, see: https://www.youtube.com/watch?v=wh4aPnI_g4I.

paradisiacal land. Let us assume that Judgment Day has brought the faithful and moral to such a land. Then, under the assumption that the inhabitants of this land are rational and under the further assumption that the political scheme by which this land is governed is infallible, in that it has perfect knowledge of the implications on the cosmos any political action incurs, I argue that the only possible governance scheme is a *dictatorship*. In fact, this is a simple implication of *Arrow's impossibility theorem*, which I briefly recount:

Gaertner (2009), Sections 1.3 and 2.1, is my reference. A preference ordering is a rational (that is, reflexive, complete, and transitive) preference relation on a set of elements, say, X. Now let X be a ground set of states of the world, let ε denote the set of preference orderings on X and let Θ be a subset of the orderings that satisfies some restriction. Let Θ^n denote the Cartesian product of 0, n times, that is, $\Theta^n = \Theta \times \ldots \times \Theta$. Such a product is a set of n-tuples of preference orderings of the form $(R_1, \ldots, R_n)$ where each R_i, $i = 1, \ldots, n$ corresponds to the preference ordering of the member i of an n-member society. A *social welfare function* (in other words: *a political governance scheme*) is a mapping from Θ^n to ε. That is, a social welfare function gives preference ordering over the states of the world by combining the preference orderings of the n members of the society. Arrow's theorem states that under the aforementioned assumptions that every individual is rational and aware of the state of the world any social welfare function brings about, then the only social welfare function that satisfies three elementary principles any reasonable collective decision process should satisfy, namely, "unrestricted domain," "the weak Pareto principle," and "independence of irrelevant alternatives" is a *dictatorship* in that a single individual dictates the preferences of the society. There are a variety of ways to escape the paradox (some more satisfactory than others):

- The inhabitants of paradise are *monads* in that their preferences coincide.

- Infallibility is impossible (even in paradise). Unfortunately, tackling this conjecture is beyond our present mathematical prowess and I believe we will remain in the dark for a while.

- Human beings do not choose rationally. In my opinion, political and economic theories are misguided in resting on the (normative) assumption that our decisions should be rational. Our theory of organization rests instead on the assumption emotions have significant influence on our decisions (and we also suggest how to abstract emotional drives in mathematical terms in the interest of rigorously proving theorems about this more complicated decision faculty).

5

ORGANIZATION BASED ON ACCOUNTABLY ANONYMOUS DELEGATION

The gold is in the dark

–Cat Pierce

An important, if not the most important, function of organization is the mechanism used to align the incentives of individual actors toward a collective effort. In this monograph, we propose to conceptually separate the *organizational actors* from the *organizational roles* they can assume, and we cast the design of incentives alignment mechanisms as problems of assigning actors to roles. A *role* directs the behavior of the corresponding actor having been assigned to that role so that he or she focuses on a part of organizational function. Roles complement each other enticing competition and cooperation in the production of goods and services. To illustrate these concepts, let us consider a motivating example.

5.1 ASSIGNING MATHEMATICAL PROBLEMS (ROLES) TO MATHEMATICIANS (ACTORS)

Consider an academic environment, say a mathematics department, where the objective is to assign mathematical problems (roles) to graduate students in the department (actors). An approach to that end is to assign the students to research advisors who then assign mathematical problems to the students. But there are alternative approaches to the same end.

Looking at an example of academic coordination between a professor and a student that panned out with minimal interaction (without involving delegation), at a group meeting of Professor Jeffrey Ullman's group in the Computer Science Department at Princeton University, Professor Ullman (2009) had an idea on *data structures* and a year later a student (outside of Professor Ullman's group) that had picked up the idea in the meeting presented Professor Ullman with a thesis on that idea. This example is suggestive of an approach to organization based on "opting for your assignment." It is thus natural to ask if we can generalize the example to a general procedure.

Coming back to the problem of assigning mathematical problems to graduate students, a way to generalize the approach of "opting for your assignment" is for the department to announce a set of mathematical problems (say, of cardinality equal to the number of students) and to ask each student for a preference ordering over these problems. To resolve conflicts, the department decides to apply a *stable marriage algorithm* to perform the assignment.

In the *stable marriage problem*, there are two sets of elements of the same cardinality. Let us assume that the first set consists of females and the second of males. Each female gives a preference ranking over the males and each male similarly over the females. The stable marriage problem is to pair males and females such that the following property is satisfied: There are no two people of opposite sex such that both prefer to be paired with the other more than their current partners.

To assign mathematical problems to graduate students using this method, the department needs to also derive preferences of mathematical problems over students. To that end, it pairs department faculty members in a one-to-one fashion with the mathematical problems in the department's list, who draw on their expertise on the skills required to solve each problem as well as on the qualifications of each student (for example, their performance in the department's qualifying exams) to provide the required preferences. A stable marriage algorithm that can perform the desired assignment is that of Gale and Shapley (1962). We build on this discussion later in the book.

5.2 BREAKING DOWN ORGANIZATIONAL FUNCTION INTO ROLES

The design of roles is beyond the scope of this monograph, but we make a few observations to that end. The first observation is that organizations can be designed in a fashion similar in spirit to a standard engineering practice of breaking down objects of design into a collection of *modules* that interact using *interfaces,* and then designing and implementing each module (along with its interface) independently. We may draw an analogy between the modular design of objects and the design of organizations (for the production of goods and services). In this analogy, organizations are the objects of design, roles correspond to modules along with corresponding interfaces (used in the interaction with other roles), interfaces correspond to the norms and formal institutions (established in the respective organization) that actors call upon to interact and cooperate, and an implementation of a module corresponds to an assignment of an actor to a role who uses his or her skills to fulfill the functions that role is meant to perform.

Our second observation is that the technique of modular engineering design has been applied to building the internet: the famous TCP/IP architecture (that the internet is based on) and the OSI (Open Systems Interconnection) reference model of building network architectures are precisely examples of modularity in internet engineering.

Our third observation is that modular design in networks is explored in the *theory of optimization decomposition* (Chiang et al., 2007), which provides a mathematical foundation for the design of network architectures. In that theory, network functions are modeled as optimization problems whose structure suggests how the function in question should be broken down into modules. Duality transformations are often used to expose modular structure amenable to distributed implementation.

Our fourth and final observation is that the architecture of conceptually separating roles and actors is similar in spirit to the paradigm of *separating of routing from routers* that is characteristic of a number of network architectures (for example, see Caesar et al., 2005; Yan et al., 2007).

5.3 ACCOUNTABLE ANONYMITY AND DELEGATION

Bad decisions, especially ones made on behalf of organizations, can give rise to conflict. But the moral, legal, and other consequences of a decision cannot be determined at the time the decision is made and implemented. For example, a law can be rendered unconstitutional in courts of justice. Since we cannot expect to predict the legal and other consequences of decisions at the time these are made, we need effective means to localize problems in the decision-making process.

For example, the conclusion of The Economist magazine in the extensive investigation it undertook on the process that led to the inception of the Greek crisis in 2010 was that it was mere confusion that led the political leadership of Europe to decide the implementation of an austerity program in Greece (and other areas in the Eurozone). One is naturally justified to wonder if the political decision leading to the austerity programs can be rebutted.

In this monograph, we advocate going a long way beyond merely keeping accountable records of the proceedings of how decisions are made in organizations and, in this vein, we present methods that proactively influence the decision-making processes. In this vein, we've already discussed how hierarchical organization imposes an unaccountable presence of organizational actors within the professional environment of other actors (lower in the hierarchy). To counteract this phenomenon, our goal is to create accountable boundaries between actors. Our design is centered around a dual of unaccountable presence we call *accountable anonymity* that strikes a balance between accountability and anonymity.

To make a case for accountable anonymity consider modern day Greece in the era of crisis: It is often the case that arguments making perfect sense are often discredited and even silenced on dubious grounds, a practice encouraging discursive discourse oriented around profanities – this style is obvious in news programs on television but it is worth pointing out that discursive discourse occasionally emerges even in parliamentary debate. In contrast, accountable anonymity is perhaps less so important in the United States, where valuable arguments, for example, in political discourse and debate, are better off being eponymous (to grant proper credit to the contributor) rather than anonymous. However, I am familiar with public debate wherein Warren Buffett credits anonymous letters (addressed to him) identifying operational issues in his investment organization.

Accountable anonymity is important in elementary institutional functions of a democracy such as voting. Although there are parliamentary procedures where voting is eponymous, what is typically the case is that voting is anonymous. In this monograph, we are particularly interested in the decisions determining the assignment of roles to actors and, to that end, our goal is to design accountably anonymous *delegation systems*. To that end, we present the design of two delegation systems, one where assignment decisions are made by an algorithm and one where the assignment of roles to actors depends on an evaluation system conducted by peers in an anonymous fashion to ensure the quality and objectivity of evaluations in a collegiate environment.

5.3.1 Limitations of Anonymity Without Accountability

Making anonymous assignments without a credible account of the reasons, these assignments were rendered can undermine the institutional foundation of an organization as corrupt payments are not accountable. Note that hierarchies have a limited accountability mechanism in place: A position in the hierarchy and the assignments made to the corresponding actor holding that position are accountable to another actor belonging to a higher place in the hierarchy. But, as discussed earlier, the accountability of decisions at the top of the hierarchy is at stake in hierarchical organization.

5.3.2 Limitations of Accountability Without Anonymity

The right to privacy should be fundamental in all organizational ventures. To illustrate this point, consider the development of software: Software can be released by either one of two modes (approaches), namely, as an *executable* or as *open source*. Open source software can be more reliable capturing in the release, beyond the interface that is necessary to execute (use) the software, the thought process of software developers and the implementation of that interface rendering the implementation open to public scrutiny, but the code transparency has limitations (e.g., the code can be easily copied and modified without paying due credits to the software developers).

Extrapolating this tradeoff to the realm of *information products* the analogue of executable software can correspond to an opaque piece of legislation or a funding decision by the ministry of finance. Transparency can subject such information products to public scrutiny. But is transparency a first order objective of, say, governance? The answer is no: Transparency can be highly problematic in practice especially as far as governmental functions are concerned where privacy is important if not absolutely necessary (cf. diplomacy). The primitive of *accountably anonymous communication* is intended to roughly emulate transparency with minimal, or no, if possible, sacrifices in privacy.

5.3.3 Specification of Accountable Anonymity

An accountably anonymous message (for example, a decision) is a message (for example, in digital form as a sequence of characters) along with a pseudonym, a mechanism that irrefutably links the message to the pseudonym, a mechanism that links the pseudonym to an organizational formation, and a mechanism by which the organizational formation can be queried on the contents of the message such that the queries and the responses can be presented as evidence in a judicial authority. The implementation of these mechanisms can be far from trivial as the following examples illustrate.

5.3.4 Examples of Accountable Anonymity

An anonymous solution to a mathematical riddle is credible (for example, if the solution can be readily verified to be correct) but the extent to which it satisfies our definition is questionable. In the film *Good Will Hunting*, Will Hunting (Matt Daemon), a mathematical genius that is a janitor at MIT, anonymously gives an impressive solution to a mathematical riddle (an open question posed by an instructor in class) on a blackboard in a corridor.[1] The blackboard inscription is an accountably anonymous message to the extent Will can get credit for the solution.

Before exploring a general (and rigorous) method by which "eccentrics" such as Will Hunting can, in principle, irrefutably prove authorship of anonymous proofs, let us remark there are less rigorous but credible alternatives to the same end. For example, a *show of hands* can discredit usurpers that plagiarize.[2] In fact, our discussion is highly reminiscent of how King Arthur laid claim to the throne of England by virtue of his ability to command the Excalibur.

Prior to claiming the throne of England, Arthur was an anonymous king, as was the case for Aragorn, in J. R. R. Tolkien's The Lord of the Rings, prior to Lord Elrond handing Aragorn the Anduril (reforged in the shards of Narsil). Accountable anonymity has an inherent ability to protect what is important, in contrast, to the inherent vulnerability of hierarchical forms of governance whose corrupting power promises *stardom*.[3]

Coming back to anonymous proofs, John Bernoulli (a famous probabilist), in receiving an anonymous proof by Isaac Newton for the solution of the brachistochrone riddle he had posed, was able to recognize the author on the spot in exclaiming *you can recognize a lion by its paw*.[4]

---

[1] See: https://www.youtube.com/watch?v=BylkoiyzZWw.
[2] This happens in a different content in the fame film here: https://www.youtube.com/watch?v=hIdsjNGCGz4.
[3] See: https://www.youtube.com/watch?v=bPiQhOeXE_Y.
[4] See: http://www.mhhe.com/math/calc/smithminton2e/cd/tools/timeline/bernoulli_1.html.

With respect to cryptography, a form of accountable anonymity (based on *message hashing*) is used in the Guy Fawkes protocol (Anderson et al., 1998) for *authentication* and *digital signatures*.

5.4 A COMPUTATIONAL CHALLENGE IN THE DESIGN OF DELEGATION SYSTEMS

The organizational processes that assign roles to actors ought to meet as many as possible of the design requirements we put forth in chapter 3. But a further algorithmic challenge in the design of such processes is that there are $n!$ possible assignments of roles to actors, where n is the number of actors (roles). Thus, delegation systems ought to look for and exploit additional computational structure such that searching in the space of possible assignments becomes tractable.

5.5 ACCOUNTABLY ANONYMOUS DELEGATION BASED ON ONLINE LEARNING

In this section, we cast the assignment of roles to actors in an organization as a problem in theoretical machine learning. We make no statistical assumptions neither on the performance of actors nor on the valuation of the output (for example, by the market) but rather consider learning in the non-stochastic (online) setting where parameters such as performance and valuation are chosen by an adversary acting against the organizational effort. Under the simplifying assumption that there is no coordination between roles, online learning theory furnishes robust guarantees on system performance even in this adverse environment.

5.5.1 Preliminaries: The (Offline) Assignment Problem

In the assignment problem, we have to pair n persons (actors) and n objects (roles) on a one-to-one basis. We denote the value of assigning actor i to role j by a_{ij}. We call a pairing $\{(1, j_1), \ldots (n, j_n)\}$ an assignment. We assume that the value of an assignment $\{(1, j_1), \ldots (n, j_n)\}$ is the sum $\sum_{i=1}^{n} a_{ij}$. Our goal is to find an assignment $\{(1, j_1), \ldots (n, j_n)\}$ such that its value $\sum_{i=1}^{n} a_{ij}$ is maximal. The assignment problem can be formulated as a linear program (for example, see Bertsekas, 1998):

$$\text{maximize} \sum_{(i,j) \in A} a_{ij} x_{ij}$$

$$\text{subject to} \sum_{\{j|(i,j) \in A\}} x_{ij} = 1, \forall i \in \{1, \ldots, n\}$$

$$\sum_{\{i|(i,j) \in A\}} x_{ij} = 1, \forall j \in \{1, \ldots, n\}$$

$$0 \leq x_{ij} \leq 1, \forall (i,j) \in A$$

where α denotes the set of feasible pairings. The variables x_{ij} can take on one of two values, namely, either 1, if i is assigned to j or 0, otherwise. This linear program has solutions that output binary values for the decision variables x_{ij} without adding this integrality constraint in the formulation.

5.5.2 A Paradigm of Organization as an Online Assignment Problem

Our goal in the theory of organization we develop is to build a foundation for the design of systems that learn and exploit the most desirable assignments of roles to actors as the system evolution unfolds with time, that is, in an *adaptive online fashion*. The aforementioned assignment problem is as an example of an optimization problem where the parameters that determine the most desirable outcome are known a priori – the optimal solution can be computed in an *offline fashion*. In the corresponding online problem, these parameters are revealed to the algorithm in an incremental fashion with the evolution of the time horizon. A standard assumption in online learning is that the parameters that determine the performance of system are controlled by an adversary who may condition his or her choice of parameters in the past (that is, the adversary may be *adaptive*).

We capture these observations in a mathematical model, which we may naturally call the online assignment problem. In this model, learning by the system (which corresponds to an organization in our case) proceeds in rounds $t = 1, 2, \ldots$. In each round, the system selects a vector $x^t = [x_{ij}^t]$, where the decision variables $x_{ij}^t \in \{0,1\}$ satisfy the constraints of the offline assignment problem. That is, x^t is an assignment of roles to actors. The adversary simultaneously selects a vector of parameters $a^t = [a_{ij}^t]$.

There are two possibilities that present themselves on what the system learns in each round. In the *full information setting*, the system learns the vector a^t. In the *bandit setting*, the system learns only the inner product $x^t \cdot a^t$.

The bandit setting is more natural for our application domain as what the productivity would have been had the system chosen a different assignment is information falling outside the purview of organizational systems: Since mathematical models of human efficacy in organizational tasks is elusive, the productivity of an individual at an organizational task is a priori unpredictable, and, thus, a parameter we have to learn as the production work is carried out.

In the online assignment problem, the goal of the system is to minimize a quantity called *regret* defined as the difference between the value of assignments the system selected over time and the value of the best fixed assignment in hindsight. That is the goal is to minimize

$$\sum_{t=1}^{T} a^t x^t - \max_{x} \left\{ \sum_{t=1}^{T} a^t x \right\}$$

where T is the time horizon. The main concern in designing algorithms for choosing assignments from round to round is to guarantee the regret goes to zero as the length T of the horizon increases, as fast as possible.

The online assignment problem befits modeling organizational tasks where there is *no coordination* between roles in that the contribution to the value of the output at time t of assigning actor i to role j at time t is independent of the assignment $x^t = [x_{ij}^t]$. There are organizational tasks that naturally fit this model. For example, in the aforementioned example of assigning mathematicians to mathematical problems, a natural assumption to make is that the mathematicians will keep their work private before publication. But note that our learning model can capture cooperation in *autonomous groups* (which is the norm in academic and corporate environments) in a natural fashion through having both individual actors and groups participating in the assignment process.

5.5.3 An Algorithm for the (Bandit) Online Assignment Problem

Let us now discuss an algorithm for the online assignment problem of McMahan and Blum (2004) called BGA. We give pseudocode for BGA in Fig. 5.1 noting that it solves a more general problem. The pseudocode assumes that in each time period, the algorithm suffers a loss (the negative of a reward).

In the bandit online assignment problem, we have an arbitrary bounded set $S \subseteq \mathbb{R}^n$ of feasible points. The BGA algorithm is initialized with a set $B = \{b_1, \ldots, b_m\}$, called a *basis*, of at most n points in S. The basis B is a *baricentric spanner* (see (Awerbuch & Kleinberg, 2004; McMahan & Blum, 2004) for the definition and techniques to compute a baricentric spanner). At each time step $t = 1, 2, \ldots$, with probability γ BGA *explores* by playing a random basis

```
Algorithm BGA(γ, ε)

Choose a basis B = {b₁, ..., bₘ} ⊆ S.
For each t = 1, 2, ...
Toss a coin that is heads with γ and tails with 1 − γ;
if heads then
    Select xᵗ from distribution FPLₑ(l̂(1), ..., l̂(t − 1));
    Suffer loss lᵗ = cᵗ · xᵗ;
    l̂ᵗ = 0;
else
    Draw j uniformly at random from {1, ..., n};
    xᵗ = bⱼ;
    Suffer loss lᵗ = cᵗ · xᵗ;
    Let λᵗ = [λ₁ᵗ, ..., λₘᵗ]ᵀ such that λᵢᵗ = { (m/γ)lᵗ,  i = j;
                                                0,        otherwise;
    l̂ᵗ = (Bᵀ)⁻¹λᵗ;
endif
```

Fig. 5.1. Pseudocode of Algorithm BGA.

element and, otherwise, the algorithm *exploits* by playing according to the Kalai-Vempala algorithm that solves the following online problem in the full information setting: At each time step t, an online algorithm selects a point $x^t \in S$ and simultaneously an adversary selects a cost vector $c^t \in \mathbb{R}^n$. The algorithm then observes c^t and incurs cost $x^t \cdot c^t$. Kalai and Vempala (2005) show that for as long as we have an efficient algorithm for the *offline* problem (given $c \in \mathbb{R}^n$ find $x \in S$ to minimize $c \cdot x$) and for as long as the cost vectors are bounded, we can efficiently solve the online problem of performing nearly as well as the best fixed $x \in S$ in hindsight. In the pseudocode, FPL (Follow the Perturbed Leader) is a subroutine calling the Kalai-Vempala algorithm using the estimates of the loss vectors BGA computes. We note that BGA achieves zero per-round regret as the time horizon approaches infinity, where the regret is defined with respect to the best fixed feasible point of S. In the bandit online assignment problem, S is the set of all possible assignments and m is at most n^2, where n is the number of actors. Since the offline assignment problem can be solved efficiently in polynomial time, we can apply the Kalai-Vempala algorithm to solve the online assignment problem in the full information setting. Thus, we can use this algorithm as a subroutine in the BGA algorithm, and, therefore, BGA can solve the online assignment problem in the bandit setting achieving zero per-round regret as the time horizon approaches infinity.

5.5.4 Benefits and Limitations

Our online learning system is an archetypical model of how to design and analyze systems that maximize joint productivity in a fashion that is robust to errors and faults in the production process in that it learns and exploits the most productive assignments and operates, by design, such that it is competitive even against an adversarial selection of parameters. Furthermore, our system can approximate rational justice as it learns for each round an approximation of the value of every possible assignment of a role to any given actor. Operating under the assumption that the value of the output in any given round is the sum of the values of the corresponding assignments having been made at that period, to achieve rational justice we can credit the actors with the values corresponding to their assigned roles. But our system has limitations: First, there is no mechanism to evaluate and take into account how the actors feel about the roles that have been assigned to them. There is naturally a correlation between productivity and the emotional content that manifests due to the production process; however, there is no explicit method for the emotions that manifest to affect the assignments. Second, although exploration is an integral part of the system, it is performed in a mechanistic fashion that is beyond the influence of the actors. Designing an online learning system that corrects these limitations is an interesting question for future work.

5.6 ASSIGNING ROLES THROUGH A DEMOCRATIC DELEGATION SYSTEM

The aforementioned online learning method for assigning roles to actors rests on a measurement of the value of the output of the production effort and through a mechanistic process searches the space of feasible assignments so as to maximize the value of the output over time. In that system, actors influence the evolution of assignments in the time horizon of the production effort indirectly, that is, only through their performance in their respective roles having been assigned to them by the system. In this section, we consider an alternative set of techniques for our assignment problem where actors have direct influence over how the assignment is performed. The system we propose (one based on evaluations by experts or peers) is presented incrementally. Its main characteristics are that it makes use of cryptography to protect the privacy of the evaluations that it aggregates multiple evaluations using a rank aggregation algorithm, and that evaluations are partial capturing overlapping subsets of the organization. The value of the output of the production process is factored in reassignments through the direct judgment of coworkers but also through "election campaigns" where candidates have the opportunity to present their work to a wider audience in the organization.

5.6.1 Accountably Anonymous Delegation Based on Cryptography

Recall the example in Section 5.1 where a group of graduate students must be assigned to mathematical problems. In the example, each mathematical problem is assigned to a professor who ranks the students according to his or her perceived ability of excelling at that problem. It would be desirable in the interest of obtaining objective evaluations and fostering an amiable collegiate environment not to disclose the professor rankings to the students (or possibly other faculty members). A strawman approach to meet this requirement is for students and professors to hand in the rankings to a third party (for example, the department's secretary) who will keep the rankings secret and only announce the final outcome of the assignment process. In this process the evaluations are anonymous but the process is not accountable. In a less straightforward approach it is possible to use cryptography, in particular, a *secure multiparty computation* system instead. For example, the algorithm of Goldreich et al. (1987) can compute the desired assignment using the Gale-Shapley algorithm without any student or professor disclosing his or her rankings to any other student or professor under minimal assumptions (that is, an honest majority of parties).

5.6.2 Combining Multiple Rankings per Role

A limitation of the previous assignment method is that each problem has a "perspective" over students determined by the ranking of a single professor. If we can expand these perspectives by obtaining rankings from more than one professor that share expertise in a particular area, then the quality of matching students and problems can, in principle, be improved. To apply the Gale-Shapley algorithm, we must first *aggregate* the respective rankings for each problem. In the *rank aggregation problem*, we are given a set of rankings and the goal is to compute one aggregate ("average") ranking. To that end, we may define a *measure of distance* between rankings and define an aggregate ranking to be one which minimizes the sum of the distances to the individual rankings. The aggregate ranking that is computed thus depends not only on the definition of distance but also on the algorithm used to perform the aggregation. Frequently used measures of distance are the *Kendall tau distance* and the *Spearman footrule distance*. An aggregation obtained using the Kendall tau distance is called a *Kemeni optimal aggregation* – the problem of computing such an aggregation is *NP*-hard. Instead, an aggregation obtained using the Spearman footrule distance can be computed in polynomial time.

5.6.3 Accountably Anonymous Delegation Using Peer Evaluations

We have developed a progression of ideas in our role-to-actor assignment problem that naturally leads to the idea of performing accountably anonymous delegation using *peer evaluations*. Let us define this problem more clearly: As before, we are given a set of actors and a set of roles and the goal is to assign roles to actors in a one-to-one fashion. Each actor provides a ranking over the roles. Our goal is to obtain a ranking of actors for each role in order to apply the Gale-Shapley algorithm. One approach is to require from each actor to provide a complete ranking over all actors in the organization (including himself or herself) for each role. (These rankings would then be combined into a single ranking using a rank aggregation algorithm.) But in medium-to-large organizations, this process would be tedious and error prone (if at all tenable). In the sequel, we devise a scalable approach to the same end based on the idea of generating and aggregating *partial rankings*.

Suppose that the number of actors is n. For each role, we select a parameter m (the number of evaluations), where $m \leq n$, and we construct a directed graph $G(V, A)$ whose vertices V are in one-to-one correspondence with the set of actors and whose arcs A are chosen such that the in-degree and out-degree of every vertex is m. The graph determines how evaluations are performed: Each actor, say corresponding to vertex u, ranks the actors corresponding to the vertices $v \in V$ such that $(u, v) \in A$. This process provides n partial rankings (over the actors) of size m each that overlap so that each actor appears in exactly m partial rankings. To obtain a ranking for the role corresponding to graph G, we aggregate these partial rankings according to *rank-distance* (as a measure of similarity between partial rankings) using the algorithm of Dinu and Manea (2006). This algorithm can be executed in a privacy preserving fashion (that is, without revealing the partial rankings) in a fashion similar to how votes are secret in a democratic election process.

5.6.4 Democratic Principles at the Forefront of Professional Life

Our design is a significant departure from hierarchical delegation: Organizations adopting our system would essentially transition from a quasi-monarchy to a democratic system of organization. To earn desirable assignments, actors can influence the evaluations of their peers through the quality of their work in previous assignments but also through demonstrating professionally appealing character attributes such as integrity especially as they try to compete for new roles in the interest of expanding their credentials and experience. But we also envision that such "democratic organizations" will promote an analogue of election campaigns in the paradigm of democratic elections and enact periods where such campaigns can take place in a formal setting. In these campaigns, formal presentations (where actors will discuss past achievements and outline future goals) could act as a venue toward the end of influencing coworkers to produce favorable reviews. Other related mechanisms such as an *organizational billboard* where organizational members, for example, post evaluations of their colleagues (possibly in an accountably anonymous fashion) could serve the same end.

5.6.5 Benefits and Limitations

A basic characteristic of our system is that it is designed around aligning possibly conflicting *human preferences* using *human appraisals* (in a process that resembles how democracy operates through progressing elections). Although, this system provides no analytical performance guarantees (in that there is no tractable underlying model to perform mathematical analysis), all design requirements laid out in Section 3 factor in the assignments made: (1) The preference orderings obtained in the peer evaluation process capture in a single evaluation a combination of parameters such as the productivity of an actor in a role, his or her fallibility in that role, and the emotional content that manifests due to the production process (and how that affects the respective actor's environment). (2) What's more, actors can perform a self-appraisal through their preference orderings. For example, if the productivity of an actor is low at a particular role, that actor would naturally wish to downgrade that role in his or her preferences. (3) Furthermore, the process of exploring the space of assignments is guided by what roles actors wish to explore: Actors that wish to explore new roles can ramp up the ranking of these roles in their preferences. But these decisions have to measure up to how well the evaluation system thinks these actors would perform in new assignments. (4) Finally, rational justice can be rendered through a democratic process of human judgment based on an evaluation of the contribution of peers in the final output in a fashion similar to how the rankings are obtained in the role assignment process.

6

CONCLUDING REMARKS AND FUTURE WORK

One of the goals of this monograph is to lay the foundations of a theory of organization where the actor is a first order principal of the organizational system (rather than a resource of the organizational apparatus). To that end, it is worth looking into a paradigm shift in the design of computing systems that was pronounced as the internet emerged as a global communications platform.

The first computers (the precursors of modern computing devices) were voluminous and expensive machines that required a significant budget from an organization to acquire. Computer protocols (implemented in those machines' operating systems) were oriented toward maximizing device utilization: Computing was oriented toward hardware at the expense of the human operators that coordinated access to computing devices and at the expense of computer programmers.

The evolution of processor technology according to Moore's law drove a decline in the size of computing equipment and in the cost of computing, and the value of the software developer started to stand out as being more significant than the value of the equipment. Such change in perspective was followed by a paradigm shift in the desgn of software that became user friendly.

The advent of the internet had a similar effect: The first research proposals requesting funding for the ARPANET (the precursor to the internet) were proposing to build a network to facilitate remote access to supercomputing centers. However, it was the proliferation of social applications (such as email) that drove an increase in traffic to justify further investment in networking research and infrastructure (Abbate, 1999). Eventually, computer programmers and internet users became first order principals of the computing and networking infrastructure of the internet.

As we transition from the *industrial age* (driven by the value of manufacturing equipment) to the *information age* (driven by the value of information in decision-making processes), it is natural to ask if we can extrapolate the evolution in computing and the internet to the design of organizations. To that end, in this monograph, we proposed a theory of organization aiming to place those that contribute to the production of goods and services as *first order principals* of organization.

The greatest challenge in doing the research required for writing this book was to maintain a cognitive equilibrium in staying true to principles I did not have the chance to formalize prior to testing them in practice. That is, in writing this book, I realize I have stayed true to principles that not only admit clear formulations but also exhibit explanatory consistency in their interactions, principles I did not know they were there ahead of time.

I have, thus, empirically tested a large variety of ideas in this book in a world that has largely been resistant to accepting them so far. That my perspective is meaningful from a theoretical perspective implies others can more easily investigate the extent to which they can influence it (through theoretical and empirical work) and adopt it (in organizations, as citizens, and as employees). Some of the work that would be required to shifting the mindsets of other people to more rigorous and, why not, mathematical perspectives of society do not necessarily imply one has to go through the suffering I went through. In attending the COLT conference in Haifa in 2010, a speaker had mentioned that Condorcet died because of his theoretical mindset.[1] I am fortunate I am alive. This constitutes empirical evidence that my organization theory is incrementally deployable. But this is partial evidence and further work is required to study it from this perspective.

The reasons for maintaining my cognitive equilibrium can be traced to a variety of factors, which I take the opportunity to discuss. First and foremost is my Greek education and upbringing. I have always been proud I am Greek and I have often defended my identity outside of Greece at the expense of a variety of other things. But I only feel partially Greek anymore and this is key: In the United States, whose culture has influenced and successfully laid claim to the other part of my present identity, I intellectually grew as a person in a fashion complementary to what I had felt was missing but also in other ways I hadn't imagined and were great fun to pursue.

For example, complementing education with an industrial perspective, an essential part of the academic curriculum in Computer Science (CS), has

---

[1] In my opinion, out of the depths of my intuition, Pavel Urysohn could have died on similar grounds.

influenced me greatly. An internship at Akamai Technologies during my first summer in America has not only been in my heart since then but still continues to shape my mathematical work even to this day by virtue of discussing with important intellects bent on solving practical problems that is so characteristic of American thinking. I hope this spirit will have the opportunity to flourish in Greece sooner or later.

There is a third crucial aspect to the stability of my equilibrium and that is no other than *mathematics,* which I essentially had to study in depth myself over a long period of years as I was leaving Princeton on my way to Berlin, throughout my stay in Berlin, and then again as I came back to Athens. This study was done at the expense of writing academic papers and without guidance other than what I wanted to study most. But it was crucial: I recall discussing with an academic colleague that studying sophisticated math of any kind along with a research problem, even if that problem is not necessarily mathematical, creates an *aquiline pupil* as you attack. I did not use the word aquiline pupil back then, but it certainly seems apposite.

Something that had deeply troubled me, however, back then and still continues to bother me now, as I have not yet been able to find the answer, is this: The schema of *attacking* mathematical problems is adopted by many theoreticians. For example, a fellow academic had mentioned the phrase *sinking one's teeth into a problem* in private communication. What is thus bothering me is the extent to which this cognitive schema of an attack is essential to mathematical problem-solving, whether a female intellect can resonate with this perspective and, otherwise, what other cognitive schemas of problem-solving would be more befitting for female elegance in the interest of creating an inclusive mathematical culture. I am looking to dispel the stereotype of females nurturing (mathematical) genius, but my work to that end is still in the making.

I believe the combination of these things, namely, the Greek culture, the American culture, and the culture of a theoretical perspective on life is worth exploring further. I feel that the glory of the *golden age of Pericles* we celebrate in school has transpired to America in a fashion different from the way it has transpired to modern Greece and that, in fact, these views are complementary. As for whether theory is important, I am not the right person to advocate its significance.

Let me finally say that my environment's tacit promise I am not alone has been crucial and add that "raw hierarchies" may have a role to play in the governance of our organizations but my conjecture is that this role is going to be marginal if at all meaningful.

6.1 MATHEMATICAL PROBLEMS IN COGNITION AND COMPUTATION

6.1.1 On the Importance of Real Numbers for Computational Complexity

I conjecture that without the real number system (that is, without using results whose proofs rest on the construction of the reals), resting only on results that rely on the rationals, we have $P \neq NP$. I believe that separations in the complexity of problem-solving in the pattern of the conjecture could have applications in artificial intelligence (AI) (to limit the reasoning capacity of robots).

6.1.2 On the Study of Emersions

I believe that the understanding of emersions will benefit from the study of *spontaneous reactions* in mathematical philosophy.[2] These are reactions that do necessarily result as the outcome of an action on the system generating them. Spontaneous reactions are related to the *Thomson lamp*.[3] In this vein, I conjecture that the Thomson lamp is undecidable with a Turing machine.

6.1.3 On the Dual of a Turing Machine

I conjecture a dual of a Turing machine exists that is a *finite-dimensional variational inequality problem* (which is an equilibrium problem over a vector field; for example, see (Facchinei & Pang, 2003)) that discrete algorithmic problems can have continuous duals is argued by the *max flow min cut* duality in graph theory. This approach to understanding computation can lead to generalizations of the Turing machine based on (duals of) infinite-dimensional variational inequalities.

6.1.4 The Quest for Mathematical Dualisms

One of the main characteristics of the human brain is that it consists of a pair of hemispheres (that are densely connected to each other). But the function of

---

2 https://plato.stanford.edu/entries/spacetime-supertasks/.
3 https://rjlipton.wordpress.com/2013/04/05/zeno-proof-paradox/.

the hemispheres is not symmetrical. Such *hemispheric asymmetry* can indicate a principle of parity violation in brain function related to duality. From a mathematical perspective, pushing the relatively recent idea of duality to further frontiers can only be prolific in my opinion. To that end, I would like to discuss two ideas that are related to mathematical programming duality.

6.1.4.1. Linear Programming Duality as Negative Transposition

Robert Vanderbei in his lecture notes on linear programming[4] presents duality as *negative transposition*. Let us show the duality transformation in this format for clarity assuming familiarity with linear programming. The following linear programs are duals:

$$\text{maximize} \sum_{i=1}^{n} x_j c_j$$

$$\text{subject to} \sum_{i=1}^{m} a_{ij} x_j \leq b_i, i = 1, \ldots, m$$

$$x_j \geq 0, j = 1, \ldots, n$$

$$\text{minimize} \sum_{j=d}^{m} b_i y_i$$

$$\text{subject to} \sum_{j=d}^{n} y_i a_{ij} \geq c_j, j = 1, \ldots, n$$

$$y_i \geq 0, i = 1, \ldots, m$$

The latter linear program can be equivalently written as

$$-\text{maximize} \sum_{j=d}^{m} -b_i y_i$$

$$\text{subject to} -\sum_{j=d}^{n} y_i a_{ij} \leq -c_j, j = 1, \ldots, n$$

$$y_i \geq 0, i = 1, \ldots, m$$

The negative transposition property becomes clear as we write the primal and dual problems in block matrix form as follows:

$$\begin{bmatrix} c^T & 0 \\ A & b \end{bmatrix}$$

where A is the matrix of A_{ij}, b is the vector of b_i, and c is the vector of c_j.

---

[4] https://www.princeton.edu/~rvdb/542/lectures/lec5.pdf.

6.1.4.2. Changing the Meaning of Negation

The negation operation in viewing linear programming duality as the negative transposition of a matrix that represents the linear program can be viewed at more abstractly as taking the *additive inverse* in the algebraic field of real numbers. This raises the natural question of exploring duality transformations based on the *multiplicative inverse* of matrices that represent linear programs. It is also worth pondering to what extent Vanderbei's perspective can be extended to *nonlinear programs* such as ones in *convex optimization* (where the objective function and constraint set are convex).

6.1.4.3. Changing the Meaning of Zero

That zero should be a number was not a definitive assumption in mathematics before Ptolemy (who is known to have tinkered with the idea). In algebraic fields, zero is the only number that is the additive inverse of itself. In my opinion, there are prolific ways of understanding nature under different assumptions on the meaning of zero: Algebraic fields have a notorious exception, namely, that zero is the only element that does not have a multiplicative inverse. This begs the question whether number systems where zero is both the additive and multiplicative inverse of itself exist. Should zero be topologically connected to infinity then? How does duality change under this assumption?[5]

6.2 A MATHEMATICAL FORMALIZATION OF ACCOUNTABLE ANONYMITY

The notion of accountable anonymity (that the delegation systems we present in this monograph are based on) is a dual of unaccountable presence. We believe there is a transformation that can make the relationship between accountable anonymity and unaccountable presence mathematically precise.

---

5 In the course of mathematical research that led to results of interest in this chapter, I posted a manuscript (https://arxiv.org/abs/1609.08934) that has an error: I inadvertently assumed (analytical) continuity of a function at infinity. But, in the real numbers, infinity essentially amounts to *nowhere* thus my algorithmic technique and proof is rendered incorrect. On the grounds that there exist fields under which zero is topologically connected to infinity, it is worth pondering to what extent my algorithmic techniques in that manuscript are, perhaps automatically, corrected.

In fact, accountable anonymity is an extremal instance of the more general notion of *accountable boundaries*. We believe such spectrum can also be studied from a mathematical duality perspective.

6.3 A MATHEMATICAL MODEL OF EMOTIONAL SYNTHESIS

Elementary mathematical reasoning suggests that it is a computational process that synthesizes emotions, for if our definition of computation did not capture emotional synthesis, we could extend our definition of computation to capture that process. However, the computational model by which this synthesis happens is an important desideratum, I believe, in the theory of computation. Turing, in devising his model of computation, tried to capture in rigorous terms, the process of solving problems using paper and pencil (cf. (Goldreich, 2008)). The synthesis of emotions does not seem to fall under the purview of such a process. Further work is, thus, required to understand the process of emotional synthesis from both a computer science and a cognitive science perspective.

6.4 A RESEARCH CHALLENGE IN ARTIFICIAL MOTIVATION

Impressing artificial motivation in computers becomes interesting as we consider AI systems. It may be possible to build autonomous intelligent computational systems whose behavior is contingent on conditions that mimic human motivation. But the extent to which artificial motivation can act as a substitute for human motivation in organizational tasks performed by AI systems is unclear. Note that the ability to motivate a computing system to autonomously perform a crime is something researchers and practitioners in AI should be worried about as autonomous AI is deployed in the field.

6.5 A RESEARCH CHALLENGE IN MEDICAL SCIENCE

Medical science seems to downplay the role of the psyche in therapeutic treatment focusing instead on pharmaceutical therapies. We believe the reason is the confluence of economic factors. For example, improving working conditions can be more expensive than purchasing and providing a corresponding health insurance program focused on treatment using medication-based therapy. In this fashion, the medical profession enables businesses and corporations to outsource employee health to medical doctors and hospitals that financially benefit from this implicit agreement. This schema of implicit collaboration between businesses and doctors creates positive externalities in the study and research into the somatic aspects of disease and sidetracks efforts that focus on the psychic (mental) aspects. I hope that this book will be used to incite and instigate efforts in the direction of exploring the apparent duality between soma and psyche I advocate in Chapter 2.

REFERENCES

Abbate, J. (1999). *Inventing the Internet*. MIT Press.

Anderson, R., Bergadano, F., Crispo, B., Lee, J.-H., Manifavas, C., & Needham, R. (1998). A new family of authentication protocols. *ACM SIGOPS - Operating Systems Review*, 32(4), 9–20.

Awerbuch, B., & Kleinberg, R. (2004). Adaptive routing with end–to–end feedback: Distributed learning and geometric approaches. In *Proceedings of the 36th Annual ACM Symposium on Theory of Computing (STOC'04)*, pp. 45–53.

Bertsekas, D. P. (1998). *Network optimization*. Athena Scientific.

Blaug, R. (2014). *How power corrupts*. Palgrave Macmillan.

Caesar, M., Caldwell, D., Feamster, N., Rexford, J., Shaikh, A., & van der Merwe, J. (May 2005). Design and implementation of a routing control platform. In *Proceedings of the Networked Systems Design and Implementation*.

Carson, S. (2011). The unleashed mind. *Scientific American Mind*, 22, 22–29.

Chiang, M., Low, S. H., Calderbank, A. R., & Doyle, J. C. (2007). Layering as optimization decomposition: A mathematical theory of network architectures. *Proceedings of the IEEE*, 95(1), 255–312.

Cormen, T., Leiserson, C., & Rivest, R. (1990). *Introduction to algorithms*. MIT Press.

Dinu, L. P., & Manea, F. (2006). An efficient approach for the rank aggregation problem. *Theoretical Computer Science*, 359, 455–461.

Facchinei, F., & Pang, J.-S. (2003). *Finite–dimensional variational inequality and complementarity problems*. Springer-Verlag.

Gaertner, W. (2009). *A primer in social choice theory*. Oxford University Press.

Gale, D., & Shapley, L. S. (1962). College admissions and the stability of marriage. *American Mathematical Monthly, 69*, 9–14.

Goldreich, O. (2008). *Computational complexity: A conceptual perspective.* Cambridge University Press.

Goldreich, O., Micali, S., & Wigderson, A. (1987). How to play any mental game. In *Proceedings of the 19th Annual ACM Symposium on Theory of Computing (STOC'87)*, pp. 218–229.

Hardin, G. (1968). The tragedy of the commons. *Science, 162*(3859), 1243–1248.

Kalai, A., & Vempala, S. (2005). Efficient algorithms for online decision problems. *Journal of Computer and System Sciences, 71*, 271–307.

Laffont, J., & Martimort, D. (2002). *The theory of incentives: The principal–agent model.* Princeton University Press.

Langner, C. A., Epel, E. S., Matthews, K. A., Moskowitz, J. T., & Adler, N. E. (2012). Social hierarchy and depression: The role of emotion suppression. *Journal of Psychology, 146*, 417–436.

McMahan, H. B., & Blum, A. (2004, July). Online geometric optimization in the bandit setting against an adaptive adversary. In *Proceedings of 17th Annual Conference on Learning Theory, COLT 2004*, Banff, Canada.

Nash, J. F. (1950, January). Equilibrium points in n–person games. *Proceedings of the National Academy of Sciences, 36*(1).

Nash, J. F. (1951, September). Non–cooperative games. *The Annals of Mathematics, Second Series, 54*(2), 286–295.

Pinker, S. (1997). *How the mind works.* W. W. Norton.

Sandholm, W. H. (2010). *Population games and evolutionary dynamics.* MIT Press.

Skyrms, B. (2004). *The stag hunt and the evolution of social structure.* Cambridge University Press.

Strauss, N. (2005). *The game: Penetrating the secret society of pickup artists.* Regan Books.

Strichartz, R. S. (2000). *The way of analysis.* Jones and Bartlett.

Ullman, J. D. (2009). Advising students for success. *Communications of the ACM, 52*(3), 34–37.

Williamson, D. P., & Shmoys, D. B. (2010). *The design of approximation algorithms*. Cambridge University Press.

Yan, H., Maltz, D. A., Ng, T. S. E., Gogigeni, H., Zhang, H., & Cai, Z. (2007, April). Tesseract: A 4D network control plane. In *Proceedings of the Networked Systems Design and Implementation*.

Printed and bound by CPI Group (UK) Ltd, Croydon, CR0 4YY
22/11/2023